TELEMENTAL HEALTH

The Essential Guide
to Providing Successful
Online Therapy

Best Practices ▪ Laws & Mandates
Risk Management ▪ Billing & Documentation ▪ Ethical Roadmap
Customizable Forms & Checklists

Joni Gilbertson LCPC, LMHC, BC-TMH, CTMH

All identifying information, including names and other details, has been changed to protect the privacy of individuals. This book is not a substitute for continuing education or professional supervision, or for seeking advice from a trained professional. The author and publisher disclaim responsibility for any adverse effects arising from the application of the information contained herein.

PESI
Publishing
& Media
pesipublishing.com

ABOUT THE AUTHOR

JONI GILBERTSON, MA, NCC, LCPC, LMHC, BC-TMH, is a licensed clinical professional counselor, board-certified telemental health provider, and the owner and founder of COPE Counseling Services, LLC. In her practice, she uses telemental health to assist individuals, couples, and families with coping in areas such as depression, suicide, domestic violence, relationships, and anger management. She is licensed as a mental health professional both in Illinois and Florida and presently resides full time in Florida.

Joni's passion for using technology to serve her clients inspired her to complete over twenty training classes on telehealth. She also edited sixteen online courses for telemental health. She is a certified trainer in clinical telemental health, mental health first aid, and motivational interviewing. She is also certified in domestic violence facilitation and selective other methods that enhance client awareness. She regularly uses distance counseling to work with diverse populations by using video sessions and other technologies. She started one of the first telehealth programs for court-ordered clients and has over ten years of experience with using video sessions for her clients.

Joni is an experienced supervisor of a hospital mental health staff and is experienced in supervising interns within her clinical practice. She trains mental health agencies, children and family services, first responders, and employees at jails, prisons, and detention centers on mental health topics, as well as legal and ethical matters of relative concern to each population. Joni is a recently retired college instructor who worked within the sociology department, where she designed and instructed seventeen mental health, legal issues, and criminal justice classes. During her last year at the college, she was nominated and presented with an award for "Teachers Who Make a Difference" due to her engaging and dynamic style of teaching.

Joni Gilbertson, MA, NCC, LCPC, LMHC, BC-TMH
joni.gilbertson@gmail.com

DEDICATION

To the participants in my seminars, webinars, and programs: This guidebook was written because of all of you. Your comments and questions through the years inspired me to search for answers and stay current with the latest laws and research. Your desire to gain knowledge motivated me to write this book as a guide while using telemental health to serve clients. I am so thankful for each comment and every question and the time given to bring it to my attention.

TABLE OF CONTENTS

ACKNOWLEDGMENTS

Dennis Gilbertson: For always encouraging me to go forward with my many ventures and for diligently working to help me in any way possible during the writing of this guidebook. You are my knight in shining armor.

Josh Lindblad: For believing in me and asking me to write this book.

Shelly Bastean: For sharing your time and your expertise on working with children. I believe you could write a book with your knowledge on this topic. You are brilliant.

Cristy Hasty: For your constant respect and admiration about the work I do. Your belief in me is empowering and endearing.

Cindy Brummett: For your constant faith in my ability and for your listening ear as I talked through my vision and shared my excitement for this book. You are a bright light in my life.

Jenessa Jackson: For your conscientious, thorough, and thoughtful editing. I am amazed at all the work that went into each and every comment you wrote. I am so appreciative of your assistance in keeping the integrity of this book.

Amy Forsberg and Kate Sample: For all the hard work you both put into reading and editing this book. I am thankful for your intelligent eyes on the grammar and structure.

The staff at PESI: My life is enriched because of all of you and your trust in me. I will always be grateful to each and every one of you.

INTRODUCTION

I developed this resource during a difficult time in our world, when the COVID-19 pandemic forced people to stay at home and businesses to shut down. Mental health providers could no longer see their clients in person and, in turn, were faced with difficult decisions. Many began considering the use of technology to meet the needs of their existing clients and provide services in a physically safe manner. Other providers were not so sure due to the complexities of setting up a telehealth practice, or they were reluctant to do so for other reasons, such as a lack of understanding in this area. However, professionals who were not interested in using technology were faced with the possibility of closing their doors and referring their clients elsewhere. Many chose the best-case scenario, which was to learn about how they could use technology so they could add video conferencing as an option for their clients, in addition to meeting with them in person when business doors reopened and in-person sessions resumed.

Given that some clients needed treatment to survive during this time, tensions were high as professionals searched for solutions. If clinicians were to stop seeing clients while the doors to their business were closed, ethical issues (such as client abandonment) arose. But for clinicians who had never used technology to provide treatment, lack of competency was also a concern. At that time, I was traveling and presenting on the law and ethics of using technology, and I was also seeing clients at my home office via virtual video sessions, so the transition was somewhat smooth for me. But for many, it was not. It was clear that clinicians who had never used video sessions with their clients needed guidance.

Where I live in the state of Florida, individuals were ordered to stay at home and travel was deemed unsafe, so my travel and speaking engagements completely stopped. When that happened, mental health professionals began taking the online version of my educational seminar regarding the use of telemental health (TMH), and I started getting numerous daily emails with questions on what to do and where to look for answers. That is when I decided to use the extra time at home to compile information that would assist clinicians in finding those resources.

I remember when I first started transitioning to TMH, I conducted a lot of research to determine best practices, and I also did a lot of online research. Within those searches, I found manuals that were written for telemedicine and for telehealth, but not specifically for TMH. It was difficult to find resources that gave me practical information to make to the necessary changes when using technology.

In fact, while there is a wealth of information available on telehealth, safe practices, and how to conduct effective therapy from a distance, it is sometimes difficult to know how to find relevant information that gives appropriate legal and ethical direction. I wrote this guidebook to give mental health professionals many of the basics in one location. It provides resources regarding TMH, along with case studies and scenarios to assist in the learning process. My main focus is to provide you with guidance on the clinical, technical, and administrative safeguards needed to conduct TMH, as well as ethical issues related to the use of technology when providing virtual services to clients.

In addition to practical information on privacy and security measures, I describe how a single clinician, or a group of professionals, can set up a practice using technology to provide therapeutic services from a distance. I wrote this material based on the current laws, the code of ethics, and best practices at the time of this writing. I also reviewed and incorporated other guidelines written by professional boards, as well as federal and state laws, within this book. Keep in mind that the guidelines in this document are not meant to be inflexible requirements of practice. They are also not designed, nor should they be used, to establish a legal standard of care.

Each clinician should take the necessary steps to ensure compliance with federal, state, and local laws that apply. Given that the world is rapidly changing the way we do business, it is also important for clinicians to keep in mind that the laws and best practices are also changing. New technologies are being introduced, and more clinicians are incorporating their treatment practices from a distance. Laws are changing to accommodate these new practices, which are being implemented for the protection of our clients and for our protection. Be advised that no part of this document should be taken as legal advice. It is written to assist you on your journey of using more technology in your practice and to guide you through the process of understanding the necessary factors to have in place when using technology for treatment.

This book is meant only to provide clinicians with guidance and information in taking the steps necessary to use TMH for providing services to clients. I have included other resources to help clinicians continue setting up an ethical and legal practice using TMH. The guidelines I present here simply address how professionals and clients can communicate with the use of technology, such as computers with webcams, mobile devices with cameras, and the use of text messaging and email. My hope is that this information will make it a little easier to find what you need to ensure a safe and effective practice of using TMH.

> *"Do the best you can until you know better.*
> *Then when you know better, do better."*
>   —Maya Angelou

1

The Basics

This section introduces telehealth and telemental health (TMH), and it also discusses the terminology needed to understand the information shared throughout this guidebook. To inspire the use of TMH, I also review the research on the effectiveness of telehealth to increase your confidence in using technology for treatment. In addition, I present best practices in this section and throughout the book for continued success.

Case Study

CONTINUE VIRTUALLY OR TERMINATE?

You are seeing a 40-year-old client, John, in person for court-ordered domestic violence counseling. He has completed twenty-three weeks of counseling and has only three more sessions to go before successfully finishing the program. He comes in and announces that he is moving six hours away to another city in the same state where you are licensed. You have never used telehealth before, but you have used Skype. If you do not complete the last three sessions with him, he will have to start all over with someone else.

Questions to consider:

What are the ethical issues involved?

_____

_____

What are the legal issues that you need to address?

_____

_____

How do you resolve this issue with the client's best interest in mind?

_____

_____

I was faced with a similar scenario many years ago when mental health professionals were not regularly using video counseling to conduct sessions, or at least I was not aware of anyone who was. When my client, John, told me he was moving away and wanted to know what to do about his remaining sessions, I knew I was dealing with the ethical concerns of abandonment and continuity of care. At the time this occurred, Skype was the only option for video sessions. Since there were no written rules for using Skype for counseling, and since I had comfortably used it to complete reports for the court from a distance, I thought using video sessions might be a way to help John complete his program.

Based on my previous work in law enforcement, I knew I needed to draw up some legal forms to ensure John and I were protected, so I completed a new informed consent form. When John attended his next session, we discussed the content of the informed consent form, and I documented this communication. I also discussed issues of confidentiality during the session and explained what his responsibilities were for keeping sessions private. We checked to ensure our tablets were compatible and set the date for our first virtual session.

This scenario is what inspired me to consider using video sessions and to look at other situations where the use of video sessions could assist in solving problems that interfered with in-person sessions, such as bad weather and no transportation. I knew immediately this was something that could be a good resource for many different situations. However, there were other things to consider in order to practice both legally and ethically. As time went on, the code of ethics added instruction on how to ethically use technology. Federal guidelines were written, along with HIPAA mandates, and state laws were passed to instruct mental health professionals in practicing legally.

Understanding the Terminology

During my college years, it was not necessary to understand technology to the extent that we need to in today's times. Therefore, when I first started working to understand all the laws and rules about using telehealth, I had to look up several different terms. Now that the use of technology is becoming prevalent in our practices, it is important that you, too, learn specific terms to understand and interpret the laws, codes, insurance coverage mandates, and technology necessary to ensure you are in compliance.

This section includes terms that are relevant to understanding many of these topics. I will provide definitions of these terms, as well as examples to assist you in having a basic understanding of the term, and then discuss how the term applies to the use of technology in the field of mental health. This is by no means a complete list of terminology used in the field of technology, but it is important to help you interpret the information presented in this guidebook.

Telehealth is a broad term that includes many health professions and services offered. The World Health Organization (2010) defines telehealth as:

> The delivery of health care services, where distance is a critical factor, by all health care professionals using information and communication technologies, for the exchange of valid information for diagnosis, treatment, and prevention of disease and injuries, research and evaluation, and for the continuing education of health care providers, in all the interests of advancing the health of individuals and their communities.

TMH falls under the umbrella of telehealth and includes services offered from a distance by mental health professionals. Although the term *telehealth* is somewhat standardized, TMH is only one of many terms used to describe mental health services using technology. A few other terms include telepsychology, distance counseling, internet counseling, telebehavioral health, and video counseling. When TMH first began, some clinicians called it Skype therapy or Skype counseling because Skype was the only platform available. Telehealth has even been called internet therapy and online therapy. The American Telemedicine Association (ATA) uses the terms *telemedicine* and *telehealth*, so for the purpose of this guidebook, I will use these terms as well. I will also use the term *clinicians* to refer to mental health professionals from varying professions.

Telehealth and TMH describe the provision of long-distance health care services in two different locations using technology, such as computers, telephones, and tablets. You can offer these services in several ways through synchronous and asynchronous communication. Using these two types of communication, clinicians can provide care through video, telephone calls, store-and-forward telehealth, text messaging, and several other technologies. If you are confused by this terminology, let's take some time to review the definitions. The selected terms will provide the knowledge you need to read the laws, understand the code of ethics, and know what is covered by insurances. The following are some significant terms used in the field of TMH in alphabetical order:

Asynchronous: not simultaneous or concurrent in time; not synchronous. Communication that, once it is sent, can be viewed later. For example, sending an email or a text message are both examples of asynchronous communication because you send the email or text at one time, and it is accessed at a different time. The email and text message are sent and received at different times. You are reading this paragraph at a different time than I wrote it; therefore, my communication to you through this writing is asynchronous communication. You did not receive it while I wrote it.

Case Study
EMAIL AND ASYNCHRONICITY

John's probation officer sends you an email to ask if John has completed his domestic violence counseling. His probation officer writes the email at 10 a.m., and you read it at 2 p.m. This is called asynchronous communication because the time at which the message was sent and the time at which you received it are not in sync with each other. They both happened at different times.

Authentication: verifying the identity of a user, process, or device as a prerequisite to allowing access to resources in an information system; proving that a person is who they claim they are. There are many types of authentication. The most commonly used types are: things you know, things you have, things you are, and global positioning system (GPS) location identity.

- Things you know: passwords, personal identification numbers (PIN), or code words

- Things you have: tokens, smart cards, keys, or a smartphone

- Things you are: also known as biometric authentication, such as fingerprints, keystrokes, or face scans

- GPS: built in some phones and can locate where you are at all times when turned on

These are a few of the popular types of authentication used to verify a user and a location. Using one factor from each of these four categories is called four-factor authentication. Multi-factor authentication provides added security measures, and you should consider using it on all devices where protected health information (PHI) is being viewed or stored.

Avatar: an icon, picture, character, or graphic that represents a person's online identity. Using an avatar allows clients to have an online identity without revealing their real image. It is easy to understand what an avatar is when you think of or have watched movies such as *Avatar*. In the movie, the main character took on another life and name, Jake, that was different from who he was. Consider what character you might take on if you were entering an avatar treatment program. There are now computer and tablet games that allow children to take on a cartoon character as an avatar to represent who they are. Consider the Disney movie *Snow White and the Seven Dwarfs*. Just for fun, which character would you take on as your avatar? Why did you choose that character? Wouldn't this be a great way to learn about a client?

Side note: Research regarding the use of a 16-week treatment program using avatar-assisted therapy for substance use found that participants who finished the program had fewer positive drugs tests during and after treatment compared to those who did not complete the program (Gordon et al., 2017). In addition, the arrest rate during treatment was zero! Avatar treatment programs thus have great potential, especially for those who prefer to keep treatment private. Additional research is needed to provide evidence-based treatment models for the use of avatars. For now, we can only use the current research available to us when determining efficacy.

Bandwidth: the transmission capacity of an electronic-communication connection; a range of frequencies within a given band, particularly that which is used for transmitting a signal. Large bandwidth allows you to send more information in less time. Having the appropriate amount of bandwidth is necessary to ensure a quality video session. Deciding how much you need depends on how many people are using the system at the same time. For example, if one phone call or video session uses 1.5 Mbps of bandwidth, and you have four calls going on at the same time, you would need 6 Mbps of bandwidth and at least 20 percent more to handle the overhead. Mbps stands for megabits per second and is a way to measure the throughput or speed of a network. The more Mbps you have, the faster your internet.

To ensure everyone has the same transmission capacity and there is not a degradation in call quality, it is important to place the devices at similar distances to the source of the bandwidth. Sounds like we need to call on our math skills a little or, better yet, have a technology consultant on our team. Consult with a technology specialist before purchasing your equipment and your internet system because they can assess your needs and better determine what would meet those needs.

Distance site: the location of the professional at the time the service is provided. For example, if a clinician is sitting in the office providing a video session with a client on a HIPAA-compliant platform, their office is considered the distance site. When that same clinician provides a session from home, their home is then the distance site. Determine your state's definition of a distance site when providing services so you know what is legal in your state, as definitions may differ from state to state.

Domain: the last two parts of an email or web address that show the organization's name, such as gmail.com. For example, the website name is Gmail and the domain name extension is .com. You can create your own website name at whatever domain name extension you believe is appropriate. A non-profit agency might choose the website name of freecounseling.org. Rest assured that there are online companies and specialists that will help you with this when you are ready.

Encryption: the process of translating plain text data (plaintext) into something that appears to be random and meaningless (ciphertext). Some of us might remember way back when decoder rings were popular, and designing a code was as simple as using a 0 to represent the letter A and a 1 to stand for the letter B. This is what I did when playing secret agent with my brothers and sister. My sister and I had to come up with a way to communicate in code to keep information from being leaked to "the brothers." When they found anything written in code, they couldn't understand what it said, and this is ciphertext in its simplest form. HIPAA-compliant encryption is 256-bit encryption. This level of encryption is what you need when deciding on a platform or email service to use with clients.

mHealth: devices that use mobile communication technologies, including the delivery of health information, health services, and healthy lifestyle support programs. Using a telephone or tablet for treatment is considered mHealth, including the use of mental health applications (or *apps*) for treatment purposes. The use of mobile apps can help increase client empowerment and self-management by keeping clients connected with their treatment outside of the sessions. There are apps for many different concerns that can assist clients while they are away from treatment and that can add to the treatment they are receiving.

When using apps, clinicians should consider reading the small print to understand the risks and benefits of using the app so that this information can be shared with the client. There are concerns with privacy and confidentiality because apps are not usually HIPAA compliant. In addition, some apps connect with other accounts and obtain a great deal of information about the user, so this is a risk that needs to be discussed with clients.

Make sure that both you and the client are competent in using the app so it does not cause harm for either party, such as making the client feel anxious or disempowered if they go home and don't know how to use it properly. Finally, when suggesting the use of apps to clients, be sure to document the conversation about its benefits, its risks, and the client's competence in using the app, along with the therapeutic rationale for suggesting it as part of treatment.

When I use apps, I provide clients with a handout that I developed regarding the app's risks and benefits, as well as instructions regarding how to use the app. I review the handout with clients and document that conversation. Doing so demonstrates my competence in using the app because I developed the handout, and it also shows that I am ensuring my client's competence by reviewing the information with them.

When an app allows the client to share data with the clinician, this can prove even more supportive of the therapeutic process. For example, an eating disorder app can allow the clinician to track the client's food intake over a specified time frame. Another example is an app that helps with addictions, such as smoking and drinking. I once worked with a 20-year-old who told me that she was trying to quit smoking, and she found that using an app that she shared with her therapist inspired her to continue using the coping skills throughout the week. She knew her therapist was checking in with her through the app, and that kept her focused on her goals and empowered her to stay consistent.

There are many mental health apps from which to choose. The following page provides a list of some apps that clinicians can use with clients. Feel free to use this handout as a guide for clients who may be interested.

Remember to review the benefits and risks of each app and to provide instructions to the client. Document this discussion during your communication regarding informed consent, and make sure to add the therapeutic intent of using the app with the client.

Mental Health Apps

Calm: Provides stress- and anxiety-reducing meditations, sleep stories, breathing programs, and relaxing music

Headspace®: Includes activities to learn mindfulness skills and meditation

Happify®: Contains mood-training programs with games and activities to assist clients with overcoming negativity

MindShift CBT®: Designed to help with anxiety and is based on scientific studies of CBT. Provides guided meditations, allows clients to set goals and track progress, and more

PTSD Coach: A U.S. Department of Veterans Affairs app that contains self-assessment and support for positive self-talk and anger management

Recovery Record: Promotes recovery from eating disorders with the use of questionnaires to track progress and a record to monitor meals and feelings

Mood Kit®: Provides over 200 mood-improvement activities based on cognitive behavioral therapy techniques and includes a journal feature

Parenting2Go: A U.S. Department of Veterans Affairs app that helps parents develop skills for connecting with and parenting children

The Mindfulness App®: Provides guided meditations and a five-day introductory course on mindfulness

Stay Quit Coach: A U.S. Department of Veterans Affairs app that gives support and information for adults in treatment to quit smoking, including tailored plans, interactive tools for coping with urges, and motivational messages

UCSF Prime: Allows clients with schizophrenia to connect with peers and assists with tracking goals for self-improvement

What's Up: Uses cognitive behavioral therapy and acceptance and commitment therapy methods

Originating site: the location of the client at the time the service is furnished. When a client calls for a session from their home, in most cases, the client's home is considered the originating site. There are different laws concerning what is an acceptable site, so be aware of state laws where you practice and where the client is at the time of the session.

Real time: a form of sharing data or communicating where there is no perceivable delay between the time something is sent and the time it is received. This is also called synchronous communication. Video sessions occur in real time and are synchronous communication. Phone calls and some instant messaging services are also considered synchronous communication. When the people involved are sending and receiving the messages at the same time, they are in sync with each other, and therefore it is synchronous. When you attend a seminar in person or have a session with a client in person, this is also synchronous communication. You hear and receive the communication at the same time it is given or expressed.

Remote patient monitoring: the process of using digital technologies to collect medical and other forms of health data from individuals in one location and electronically transmitting that information securely to health care providers in a different location to facilitate assessment and treatment recommendations. When an app allows clients to share their information with the clinician, clinicians can remotely monitor the client's choices, behavior, and thoughts. For example, if a client uses an eating disorder app to document what they ate and how it made them feel—and the clinician can access that app to monitor the client's behavior—that is an example of remote patient monitoring.

Another example is an app that reminds the client to take their medication and that also allows the professional to monitor the activity or non-activity. Digital blood pressure cuffs, which allow patients to send their physicians their blood pressure and pulse, are also a good example of remote patient monitoring.

Store-and-forward: collecting clinical information and sending it electronically to another site for evaluation. This information typically includes demographic data, medical history, documents (such as laboratory reports), and image, video, or sound files. This type of communication reduces the need for a higher bandwidth. Sending records from one location to another through email or an electronic health record system is an example of store-and-forward communication.

Synchronous: happening, existing, or arising at precisely the same time; real-time communication that is heard at the same time it is spoken. There is no time lapse between presentation and reception. Video sessions and phone calls are both examples of synchronous communication because they happen in real time. They are both in sync with each other and occur at the same time.

Telehealth: a collection of means or methods for enhancing health care, public health, and health education delivery and support using telecommunications technologies. The Health Resources and Services Administration (HRSA) of the U.S. Department of Health and Human Services (HHS) defines telehealth as the use of electronic information and telecommunications technologies to support and promote long-distance clinical health care, patient and professional health-related education, and public health and health administration. Some examples include videoconferencing, the internet, store-and-forward imaging, streaming media, and landline and wireless communications, with services provided through audio, text messaging, or video communication technology, including video conferencing software.

Telemental health(TMH): the provision of remote mental health care services using technology to meet therapeutic needs, either asynchronously or synchronously. Examples include video sessions to treat depression or post-traumatic stress disorder (PTSD) or even phone sessions to treat clients with relationship issues. The possibilities are endless.

Uniform resource locator (URL): the address of a resource (such as a document or website) on the internet that consists of a communications protocol followed by the name or address of a computer on the network and that often includes additional locating information, such as directory and file names. An example of a URL is: http://www.Merriam-Webster.com. Merriam-Webster is the website name and .com is the domain extension.

In addition to the terminology defined in this section, you also need to know some of the commonly used acronyms when communicating via email or text message. An example is FYI. As you have already guessed, this one means *for your information*. There are hundreds of acronyms available for use, which you can easily find online. Professional documentation should not include acronyms unless they are spelled out first. As a clinician, I suggest that you do not use acronyms when communicating with clients to ensure clarity and to remain professional. Using acronyms could give the impression of a different relationship. However, it is necessary to know some of the main acronyms because your clients will use them. I have listed a few on the following page to get you started. Feel free to copy this list and have it handy for reference when conducting sessions with those who regularly use this language.

Common Acronyms

AFK	Away from keyboard
BBFN	Bye bye for now
BFN	Bye for now
BRB	Be right back
BTW	By the way
FITB	Fill in the blank
CTN	Can't talk now
HTH	Hope this helps
IMO	In my opinion
IDK	I don't know
LMK	Let me know
LOL	Laughing out loud
NC	No comment
NP	No problem
NRN	No reply necessary
OMW	On my way
TTYL	Talk to you later
TQ	Thank you
TYT	Take your time
TYVM	Thank you very much
YMMD	You made my day

A helpful website with more acronyms is www.smart-words.org/abbreviations.

Research on Effectiveness

Telehealth has been around for a while, but with the COVID-19 pandemic, the use of technology is needed more than ever. Although this has been a struggle for mental health clinicians who were not previously using TMH, the result is that many have decided to add TMH to their options for helping clients. Many clinicians have told me that telehealth is a convenient option that provides a variety of benefits. From video sessions to avatar groups, the possibilities are endless.

With the use of TMH, clinicians can set up sessions with clients in several different ways that do not necessitate being with them in person. These options increase access to care for individuals who were previously unable to receive treatment or found it difficult to get to appointments. In this section, I will discuss some of the past and recent research demonstrating that TMH is effective for live video sessions, store-and-forward communication, remote patient monitoring, and mHealth. This information gives us assurance that we are choosing to have sessions in a way that is at least as effective as in-person care.

One study examined the efficacy of internet-based mental health programs in rural regions and concluded that depression self-help and information programs can be delivered effectively by means of the internet (Griffiths & Christensen, 2007). In fact, research suggests that there is a strong culture of self-reliance and a preference to self-manage health problems among rural residents, suggesting that internet-based delivery of care for depression may increase clients' desire to participate and improve access to care.

In addition, delivering services via telehealth may have several practical advantages for clinical practice in that it may enable increased access to populations that are hard to reach, reduce travel-related costs, make scheduling appointments easier, and increase family participation in interventions with children (Tomlinson, Gore, & McGill, 2018). Psychiatric services provided through telehealth may also reduce costs and result in fewer medication errors. And even when technical errors do occur, these issues are usually easily resolved, with no significant effect on treatment outcomes.

Finally, research examining exposure-based treatment for PTSD found no significant differences between home-based telehealth and in-person practices in reducing certain symptoms of depression and anxiety (Yuen et al., 2015). This outcome supports expanding the use of new technologies to improve access to and delivery of clinical treatments for individuals with a history of trauma.

Technological Competency

The code of ethics states that professionals must be competent in their provision of services to clients and that they must only see clients within their scope of practice and competence. Merriam-Webster defines *competency* as the possession of sufficient knowledge or skills. Having the right knowledge and needed skills can ultimately affect our attitude when working with clients, so in this section, I will discuss the importance of having a competent attitude, as well as having the needed knowledge and skill set.

Case Study
MAKING THE LEAP TO TELEMENTAL HEALTH

Marie, a licensed professional clinical counselor, is seeing Anne for in-person sessions and is treating her for an eating disorder. Marie and Anne have a strong rapport that has progressed over a period of ten sessions. Anne appears to be making progress in her treatment and says she looks forward to her time each week. One day, Anne calls and tells Marie that she is unable to drive to a session because her car broke down. She will not be able to fix it for a few months, but she wants to continue seeing Marie. One of Anne's friends told her about using video sessions, so she asks Marie if this is possible. Marie has never done video sessions before. What competencies does Marie need to have?

Marie is concerned regarding her lack of competence with telehealth and the potential harm this can cause her client, but she wants to address this so she can move forward with video sessions.

Her attitude toward the use of technology is important because if she is not willing to learn how to use technology in the first place, then she may not want to work through the typical problems that arise when conducting video sessions. If she has the attitude that "it is too much to learn," then she may not want to work through the interruptions or glitches that occur. In contrast, maintaining a positive attitude toward technology can inspire the energy needed to learn new practice techniques and use the chosen technology with ease.

Marie is excited about the option of telehealth and has a positive attitude toward using a new method of delivery, so she presents positively to Anne about this possibility. As a result, Anne continues to experience confidence in seeing Marie for treatment. However, given Marie's concerns about using technology, she plans to obtain experienced consultation and even ask for temporary supervision to ensure she is using best practices. This will help her become more confident in offering this option to her clients. By seeking support from experienced professionals, Marie is ensuring that she continues to meet all the important elements within the standard of care. She documents all these important communications, which shows her integrity as she pursues further competence using telehealth with her clients. Marie's positive attitude keeps her focused on moving forward in this new venture. Next, she must make sure she has the knowledge necessary to use telehealth.

Marie will need to know how the chosen technology works and how it will enhance her practice. She will also need to know what the security risks are and how to minimize those risks. Additionally, she will need a thorough understanding of privacy, confidentiality, and informed consent issues with the use of technology. This means she must understand HIPAA standards and other laws, such as mandated reporting, duty to warn, informed consent, and how to handle emergencies. Professionals who are not trained on the use of TMH can lack understanding concerning appropriate technology options and what they need to conduct virtual sessions, which can cause harm. Since competency is defined as having the necessary knowledge and skills, Marie is making a good choice to take telehealth training that includes information in which she is lacking. For Marie to claim competency, she must also have the knowledge and training in her field of expertise.

Once Marie has the knowledge and training on how to provide TMH, as well as the knowledge and training needed to implement a specific type of treatment, she also needs certain technological and clinical skills. First, she will need to know how to access the internet and will require basic troubleshooting skills with the technology she chooses to use. It is always good to have someone nearby who can help when knowledge reaches its limit. In addition, Marie would need to know how to communicate with her clients in this new way and to do it with ease. She would need to know how to adapt her in-person communication skills and use them with the chosen technology to ensure she communicates in an effective way with her clients and other systems.

Clinicians can achieve competence in many ways. The most important is formal training and credentialing, as well as supervised practice using technology. The ATA code of ethics states that professionals must have supervised practice before using telehealth. Check your code of ethics on this important topic because they all differ. In addition to obtaining a graduate degree in your area of expertise, consultation and continued supervision can help to show integrity toward developing competency. All these things should be well documented in a file where you keep all your continuing education classes and other education received showing how you have maintained competency.

Since technology is constantly changing, reading relevant material and taking classes is another way to continue and improve competency. A good practice is to always document the date you read the literature, what the literature was, and the main components of the reading so you can demonstrate competency. Reading this guidebook can increase your awareness and understanding of many telehealth concerns, so you can even consider reading this book to be part of your competency documentation. Document all training, readings, consultations, and supervisions in your competency file. You never know when you might be called on to prove integrity in this area.

Questions to consider:

What training do you need for competence in the areas in which you want to use technology?

_____

_____

What training do you need to use the chosen technology in this area?

_____

_____

What is your backup plan to quickly resolve technical issues?

_____

_____

What do you need to set up for continued updates to maintain competence in these areas?

_____

_____

Knowing the Risks and Benefits

Benefits of Telemental Health

Telehealth became popular decades ago when doctors had to travel many miles to provide services or when patients had to drive long distances to receive services. It was not always possible to make the long trips, so to solve the problem, telemedicine was established as a means by which physicians could provide services using technology. The ATA developed guidelines for telemedicine, which stated that a physician must first establish a physician–patient relationship in person while completing the necessary assessments and examinations. When patients needed another session, the physician could see them using technology, but only after authenticating who the patient was and where they were at the time of the session.

The use of telemedicine many years ago increased access to care because it reduced distance barriers for both doctors and patients alike. This benefit is available today for mental health clinicians and is one of the reasons I started using TMH. Remember the story about John, who moved six hours away and needed to complete three more sessions for his court-ordered treatment? To send him away and say I could not finish his twenty-six-week program seemed like abandonment, even though it was his choice to move at that time. Video sessions made it much more convenient for John.

Questions to consider:

What legal and ethical issues were part of John's case study?

_____

_____

What would you have done?

_____

_____

Presently, there are many reasons mental health professionals use TMH to provide services to clients. For example, at the time of this writing, the COVID-19 pandemic prevented clients from being seen in person due to nationwide stay-at-home orders and social distancing requirements, which left mental health professionals with a huge problem to solve: How do we treat clients whom we normally see in person? Telehealth solved that problem for many clinicians as they set up online practices with their established clients. By using videoconferencing, services continued with very little delay, which showed many clinicians that TMH was a new way to provide services that was effective and solved distance problems. For many professionals, the use of TMH has become the "new normal" as they have come to realize its benefits.

Case Study
PANIC ATTACKS IN A RURAL AREA

Patrice is a concerned mother with a teenage daughter who suddenly starts experiencing panic attacks. The family lives in a small rural area where services are limited, and Patrice is having difficulty finding a psychologist who specializes in panic attacks with teens. A friend suggests that she complete an online search for a specialist in panic attacks and youth, so she does. Within thirty minutes, Patrice finds someone three hours away who specializes in working with teens with anxiety. She immediately contacts the specialist and can set up video sessions to begin within the week. Her daughter quickly obtains the help she needs and receives treatment that eliminates the panic attacks. Patrice is pleased because her daughter did not have to miss school, and she did not have to miss work during the process.

In addition to providing another way to offer sessions, TMH solves other problems. For instance, it allows clients to access specialists more quickly and to find specialists that meet their needs in many situations. We saw this happen with Patrice's case study. She needed a specialist who could help with her daughter's sudden onset of panic attacks, but she lived in a small town and was unable to find someone. By going online and searching for someone outside of her area, she was able to solve that problem. Telehealth allows many clients to start treatment earlier, which can minimize any worsening effects they may be experiencing.

Another benefit of telehealth is that some clients are unable to leave their homes for one reason or another. It may be a physical barrier or an emotional one, or maybe they have children or a vulnerable adult at home for whom they are responsible, which prevents them from leaving. These potential clients can now schedule appointments with a qualified professional at their convenience, and they can complete their treatment from the comfort of their homes.

When I had my clinic in Illinois, there were many times that the weather kept clients from coming to sessions. Icy roads and snowfall frequently resulted in unsafe driving conditions that prevented people from leaving their homes. Now with the use of telehealth, clients do not have to miss sessions. When they have a problem with transportation, they can keep their scheduled sessions with the use of telehealth. Technology definitely has many benefits.

Now that clinicians have experienced the convenience of telehealth, many are changing the way they practice by adding TMH as an option for their clients. Clients and clinicians can save money on travel expenses, and students and parents can remain on the same schedule due to the flexibility of video sessions. Young people do not have to miss school, and parents do not have to take time off from work. Even when the weather is bad, sessions can continue using TMH.

Telehealth also has another benefit in that it reduces the perceived stigma attached to receiving mental health services. Some clients do not want others to know they are seeking treatment, so seeing a professional in the privacy of their home may be just what they need to help them get comfortable with obtaining treatment. In addition, telehealth allows clients to search for providers across a greater geographical landscape than they might for in-person sessions. In turn, they can search for someone who understands their culture and their concerns, and they can find someone with whom they are comfortable. Given this combination of privacy and flexibility, clients who would normally not want in-person sessions may become comfortable enough to enter into an online therapeutic relationship and ultimately improve their life.

Telemental Health

Case Study
TELEMENTAL HEALTH CAN SAVE LIVES

Jim, a 40-year-old soldier in the Army, is deployed to Afghanistan for the second time. Jim has made a career in the Army and has only a few years left before he can choose to retire. He is an officer and still has future goals he would like to accomplish before he leaves the service. He begins having difficulties with panic attacks, high anxiety, and suicidal thoughts, so he goes to his commanding officer and explains what he is feeling. His commanding officer tells him that mental illness is a weakness and that he should get it together quickly or it could ruin his career in the service. As a result, Jim does not get the help he needs.

Months later, Jim returns home to his family in the United States and runs into an old friend. He and his friend engage in a discussion that becomes heated, and they have an argument, which results in Jim attempting to take his life. Jim ends up at the hospital and is later sent to inpatient care for two weeks. Upon his release from the hospital, he does not want to obtain treatment because he fears he will be considered weak by his fellow soldiers and his commanding officer.

A family member suggests that he look online for a treatment specialist in his state who uses video sessions and specializes in working with the military. He finds someone quickly and can obtain the treatment he needs without walking into an office. The use of videoconferencing solved the problem of perceived stigma by offering Jim private sessions outside of the base where he reported for duty.

In addition to the many benefits that telehealth offers clients, it also offers benefits for clinicians. Having an office at home costs less than paying for an office outside of the home. When I first started my practice in counseling, I opened a clinic and paid the many expenses required to do so—plus I had another office in a building on the other side of town for those who lived closer to that area. Therefore, I was paying rent at two locations. After I moved to Florida, I began seeing clients via telehealth, so I closed my agencies. It felt like a huge risk at first because I saw most of my clients in person at that time. However, given my understanding of best practices and how to minimize and eliminate risks, it became a great decision. Most of my clients were comfortable and competent using technology, and for those who were not, I referred them to a respected colleague.

Questions to consider:

How will TMH benefit your clients?

_____

_____

What do you need to ensure security and safety of client records while at home?

_____

_____

How will you ensure that you and your clients are competent to use technology for treatment?

_____

_____

Risks of Telehealth

As with any service, there are risks associated with the use of technology to meet therapeutic needs. To run a safe telehealth practice, professionals must address these risks. As providers, we must know what the risks are so we can minimize or prevent them. The risks that remain the most daunting for professionals are those associated with privacy, security, and confidentiality. Clients have a right for their information to remain private, but given all the ways that technology can compromise privacy, it is imperative that both you and your clients understand these risks.

Case Study

SETTING UP A VIRTUAL PRACTICE

Ella, a licensed professional clinical counselor, moved to another part of the state where she holds her counseling license. She had a few clients who did not want to be referred to someone else, so she decided to start using telehealth. She presently has a private practice and is the sole practitioner. She does not have a team of people to consult with for advice on how to get her telehealth practice up and running, yet she knows that she must address these risks because she just attended a continuing education class on law and ethics. She is concerned about what is in the best interest of her clients.

Since Ella has just started to consider using TMH, there are many risks she needs to work through. First, she will incur additional costs because she does not have the appropriate technology, so she will need to purchase equipment, such as a computer that has a good microphone, webcam, and processing speed. There are many choices of computers, and this takes some research on the clinician's end to find a suitable option. If Ella does not purchase a computer with a good microphone, there is the risk that low sound quality will interfere with the quality of the session itself. In addition, if the computer does not have a reliable camera, it may be difficult to maintain good rapport with her clients since they won't have a clear image of each other. Consultation with a computer expert is a good choice here.

Ella must also purchase and set up the appropriate internet service. She knows she needs internet with enough speed and data transfer so she can accommodate video sessions and file transfers, but she doesn't know how to accomplish this. Although there is a lot of information about this topic online, talking with an internet provider is the most helpful. Ella finds out that, generally speaking, if you have 25 Mbps, you should be able to have quality video calls and stream webinars.

Now that Ella is providing services from home, she will need to consider her family's internet usage as well. Her husband and son frequently enjoy online gaming, and they do not want to experience technical problems with this while she is using the internet for video calls. If they all plan to use the internet at the same time, she may need a higher speed. When setting up your service, determine how many people will be using the internet at the same time, as this will determine how much internet speed you need. More people on the system at the same time means more speed is necessary.

For the strongest Wi-Fi signal, it is best for Ella to sit as close to her router as possible. This way, there are no walls or other objects obstructing the service. Even a microwave oven can be an obstruction. The best thing to do is use an Ethernet cable and to connect the computer to the router so there are no worries about interference. Another reason to use wired internet is that it is little faster than using Wi-Fi. When I do a webinar, I always plug into my router so there is no interference. When I do a video session, I find that I don't need to do that.

Additionally, Ella might incur training costs for understanding how to use her new technology in a secure manner, as well as continuing education costs to keep up to date on any changes in technology. She is asking for consultation and guidance in these important areas. When I obtained my graduate degree, technology courses were not on the list of classes offered for mental health counseling degrees. Given that we are now using technology in most areas of our lives, there are increased risks that clinicians must address with appropriate training.

There are risks associated with text-based communications. Depending on your carrier settings and mobile device properties, the text messages stored on and sent from your device may possibly be unencrypted and vulnerable to security threats. Any text-based communications you have with a child or adolescent pose other unique risks in that parents typically have a legal right to view their children's medical records. Remember that text messages are a literal transcript of communication between you and your clients. When texting is used therapeutically, it is considered PHI, and you must take steps to protect it.

I remember when I first started using text messages. At that time, there were no laws, rules, or codes written about the use of texting for clinical purposes. The need to encrypt messages had not been discussed because, as clinicians, we were not using this method to communicate with clients yet. During this time, one of my first clients asked me if she could use texts to schedule an extra appointment, and I agreed that she could. A few weeks later, I received a text from her saying she was feeling emotional and needed a session that day. I was teaching all day, so on my break, I let her know that

I did not have an appointment open and that I would see her in two days at her scheduled session.

About an hour later, she sent a text back asking me to cancel her appointment. I knew right away that she was upset because she never canceled appointments. During my next break, I immediately texted her back and said, "As requested, I canceled your appointment. I hope you call and reschedule soon, and I hope you are okay." She then texted back a paragraph on how she was upset at my "coldness" and how I stopped caring about her. This communication was not cold and uncaring to me, but it was to her, and her experience is what mattered to me. I called her and scheduled a new appointment in two weeks to talk about this.

Question to consider:

Who bears the burden of the harm caused here?

_____

_____

What issues do you see with using text messaging?

_____

_____

What could have been done differently?

_____

_____

To answer the first question of who was at fault: It was me. Using text messaging with this client caused harm. Although it was not intentional, it did happen, and I could have avoided it. It is easy for clients to feel misunderstood when using text messaging and emails because they are unable to hear the clinician's caring tone or see the warm expressions and body language that show interest. This happens so much with text messaging and emails that the code of ethics now addresses it. The code of ethics clearly states that we must discuss miscommunications before using these types of asynchronous communications with our clients.

This dear client returned in two weeks and flopped down in the chair while asking me why I did not want to see her anymore. She also wanted to know why I thought she would not get any better. I definitely used this as a therapeutic moment to help her understand how this thinking pattern was part of her other important relationships. But I first apologized for the harm and the hurt she experienced, and I explained that we needed to have an important discussion about the possibility of misunderstandings and miscommunications going forward. She left feeling healed from the pain she experienced and with new ways of looking at her thinking. She also left with a refreshed understanding of my care and concern for her.

However, it is not just text messages that can pose risks, as harm can also occur with emails. Specific areas of concern include data leakage, platform-specific issues, and back-end servers. Like text messages, email messages are also unsecured and can be accessed by third parties. Even deleted emails may be preserved by other third parties, such as internet service providers. When a professional sends an email from an encrypted email service, there is also no guarantee that the message is safe where it has been sent. Although a complete and thorough discussion of the broad set of security issues related to the use of mobile devices in the healthcare environment is beyond the scope of the guidebook, I will discuss some ways to minimize these risks.

One way to minimize risks is to set up a HIPAA-compliant email and texting system. It is safer to use a web-based messaging system that allows you to email clients with a prompt to log in to a password-protected website to retrieve a message because it does not travel through multiple servers. The more servers that a message must go through, the more risk associated with the account. Another way to minimize risks is to educate your clients on the security risks of using emails and texting to communicate. This is an important part of the informed consent process and should be included on your forms and in your discussions with clients prior to beginning services.

Once you have completed a risk assessment and determined vulnerabilities, you need clear policies that dictate the use of the chosen technologies to communicate with clients. These policies should explain what PHI is and is not. The policies should also indicate what methods of communication are approved with clients and which are not. Indicate how you will use these communications in compliance with the laws and the code of ethics. This is part of your risk management plan, which I will discuss in greater detail in the next chapter.

Questions to consider:

How will you make your email messages HIPAA compliant?

_____

_____

How will your texting communication be secured?

_____

_____

Best Practices for Telemental Health

When setting up a TMH practice, understanding best practices can support clinicians in meeting some of the challenges that present with videoconferencing, like maintaining privacy and security and handling emergencies. Although evidence-based research should inform our knowledge regarding the best way to practice, there remains a lack of research in some areas. Therefore, when compiling this resource manual, I decided to use information from many different sources, including current research, the code of ethics written by our licensing boards, and information from experts in the field. The best practices in this section are a compilation of that research, and I have included all my sources in the resource section.

Many of the best practices for telehealth are similar to those of in-person sessions, and some specifically refer to sessions that use technology to work with clients from a distance. Although you will need to make some modifications, it is all manageable. Some skills will stay the same, while you will need to adapt others for video sessions or other forms of technology. Here is a short review of best practices using TMH practices.

One of the best practices—which remains the same whether the session is in person or conducted virtually—is that clinicians must follow the code of ethics of their profession. For most professions, the code of ethics provides valuable information on the necessary modifications to use technology for treatment. I always suggest having a copy of the code of ethics on hand so you can easily refer to it. The code of ethics is easy to read and understand, and it offers clarity on what is right and wrong. In addition, everything in the code of ethics that is related to in-person sessions still applies.

There are also best practices for storing PHI, transferring data through emails, and texting PHI. HIPAA is clear that we should address all communication that contains PHI and encrypt it with 256-bit encryption when possible. If clinicians are not able to encrypt the communication, then it is necessary to document the reason why. (Side note: When reading HIPAA guidelines, look at what is addressable or mandatory regarding telehealth and PHI, and document what you did or did not do, along with the rationale for your choice.)

Make sure you have all the HIPAA safeguards in writing before engaging in services. This is not a small task. Usually, when clinicians are working together in the same agency, there is a manual that contains this information. Each person is responsible for reading this manual because it includes information regarding the roles and responsibilities, credentials, licenses, and mandatory training necessary to provide services, and information on how business is conducted. Since there are always changes in the world of technology, this manual should also include issues related to quality improvement and how to ensure compliance with the changing laws and standards of telehealth. This manual should also describe how emergencies are handled at the agency itself and during sessions that use technology. In the next chapter, I give guidance on many of these topics in the section on risk management.

Before conducting a session using video or other technologies, you must know how to handle emergencies. In fact, an emergency plan should be in the client's file after discussing it. I recall a woman at one of my seminars who asked me what to do about a client she had. She shared that when she was doing video sessions with this client, she was always worried that her client would have a seizure and fall, so she asked for advice on what she should do.

Questions to consider:

What are the concerns?

_____

_____

What needs to happen?

_____

_____

What would you tell this clinician she needs to do?

A best practice for handling emergencies is to know where the client is at the time of each session, who their support person is, and what hospital is nearby just in case there is an emergency. You must also know the client's emotional and physical status to determine whether it is appropriate to conduct sessions with them from a distance. This information is part of the informed consent discussion you need to have with your client during the initial distance visit, making sure to document this communication for future sessions.

I strongly recommended that you never have a session from a distance without having an emergency plan. I always check at the beginning of each session to make sure that my client is at the same location they gave me at the last session. I also inquire as to whether their support person's information is still the same. Depending on the client and the stability of their relationships, this information could change between sessions. Always check! I have included two copies of an emergency plan form and a telehealth informed consent in chapter 7.

In addition, best practices dictate that we must follow all the state and federal laws for reporting abuse, neglect, exploitation, and harm. This includes laws about domestic violence and mandated reporting. These laws may differ across states, so I have provided resources in the next chapter, which discusses legal and ethical issues.

To maintain best practices, you should only see client populations whom you are trained to see, and you must work to develop cultural competence when seeing clients from different backgrounds. This means clinicians need to be able to understand and appreciate diversity among clients, as well as care enough about clients' concerns to become familiar with their practices and the environments of which they are a part. In addition, when using video sessions, it is important to check in with clients during the treatment process to ensure they are benefiting from and are comfortable using technology. After a few sessions, they may decide they would rather be seen in person or through another type of technology, and you should give them the opportunity to make that decision.

Case Study
TO DISCLOSE OR NOT TO DISCLOSE

Kishio, a 35-year-old Asian man, is in your substance abuse group. He presents as quiet, reserved, and always respectful. He attends regularly and always completes his assignments. Kishio was court ordered to the group, and if he does not complete the program, he will probably be sentenced to jail. In this treatment program, all participants must do their homework assignments and participate in the required activities to successfully finish.

This week, you inform the group that they must tell their families they are involved in drug and alcohol group treatment. You are hoping this will inspire support for your clients from their families and that it will also help them take full responsibility for their addictions. Some participants have already talked with their families, so it is not a concern for them, but others do not want to disclose this information with their families. Kishio states that he does not want to tell his family, and he is extremely concerned about what will happen with his family if he does tell them, as well as what will happen with treatment if he does not tell them.

Questions to consider:

What would you do?

_____

_____

What is the cultural concern for Kishio?

_____

_____

What changes are needed to assist Kishio?

_____

_____

How can changes happen in a structured program to meet the needs of all participants?

_____

_____

Best practices are often determined by conducting research with a specific group of people, but this research does not always consider how best practices can differ as a function of culture or ethnicity. For example, in substance abuse treatment programs, it is considered a best practice for clients to involve their family and to enlist them as a support system when possible. Although this practice is helpful for many, it does not consider how this practice may negatively impact individuals from different cultural backgrounds, where sharing this information may be harmful.

In the Asian family in which Kishio was raised, it was believed that sharing personal information with strangers brought shame to yourself and your family. Kishio tried to explain this to the treatment facilitator, but he was told that he would not successfully complete the program if he chose not to participate and complete all homework, including telling his family he was in a treatment program for substance abuse. Kishio complied and told his family because he did not want to go to jail. His family responded by telling him that he had shamed them and that they no longer acknowledged him as part of the family.

Kishio's example illustrates how harmful it can be to work with someone and not understand the cultural differences beforehand. Although we have taken cultural diversity classes in college, it is paramount that you translate this knowledge into practice by exhibiting care and concern for the populations with whom you work. When using technology, those considerations take on new meaning. For example, eye contact means different things to different people. Knowing the specific meaning it holds for your client can help you adjust the session to accommodate and assist them in feeling comfortable with you. The good news is that making these necessary modifications is quite simple with technology. A simple screen adjustment may be all you need to meet your client's needs.

There are additional modifications that you may need to make when using technology for certain populations, so a best practice is to know what these needed modifications are before agreeing to provide treatment. Clinicians providing treatment for different populations also need to be aware of each client's developmental level so they can tailor the use of video sessions in a way that is relevant to the client's lifestyle and appropriate to their age. I have included modifications in this guidebook for working with different populations, such as children, older adults, and clients in the military.

Another best practice is to only see clients within your scope of practice and to maintain the same standard of care you would when seeing clients in person. This includes only engaging in services in which you show competence and, when possible, only providing services that are evidence-based. One way to accomplish this is to keep up with the current literature. In fact, for many mental health professions, this is a requirement when following the code of ethics.

There are many online resources available where you can review the latest research on evidence-based practices, so be sure to choose websites that are credible. Find peer-reviewed journals because they publish credible information more quickly than many other sources of information on the internet. In addition, when reading research, look at who conducted the research, as that can sometimes identify a possible bias. It is quite interesting to read about the latest technology being researched and implemented because it opens new avenues to assist our clients and inspires creativity. I will discuss this in greater detail in chapter 6 when examining the future of technology.

In addition, a best practice is to clearly let clients know what the sessions cost and how long each session is before beginning treatment. I put this in my informed consent form and discuss what happens should they not show up. Since I am seeing clients from their home, they will sometimes believe the schedule is laxer than it would be for in-person sessions. It is best to discuss this with them and to make sure they are fully informed of the charges they will receive should they decide not to show up, if there are charges. In addition, let them know what your cancellation policy is as part of this discussion. I have found that putting this in the informed consent form makes it easier to have the important conversation.

It is best to have clear communication about when clients can contact you and how that communication can happen, as well as the amount of time it will take you to respond. In my informed consent form, I include information regarding acceptable types of communication, such as text messages, emails, and phone calls, and I give the amount of time it will take me to respond to each one. That way, my clients are well-informed of what to expect, and they know how and when to contact me.

When using technology, it is a best practice to have HIPAA-compliant platforms, emails, and messaging. It is also best practice to have a backup plan when the technology fails. Again, this is part of the informed consent discussion. Along with HIPAA compliance, clinicians must have policies and procedures on how to maintain the HIPAA safeguards that are necessary to keep everyone safe.

Finally, it is a best practice to ensure that there is privacy at your location and at the client's location when a session is in progress. One of my clients who was receiving domestic violence counseling through video sessions informed me that his 3-year-old daughter was going to be in the room during our session. I reminded him about our written informed consent agreement, as well as our discussion about the sessions being private, but he was adamant that she would not be a problem because she would be watching cartoons. I handled this by reminding him of our initial agreement, and we followed by rescheduling his session. He was still responsible for the time scheduled and was not happy about it, but because he recalled the informed consent and the discussion, he knew it was the right way to proceed. It is always a best practice to have these important discussions prior to beginning treatment. Be sure clients are informed when they consent. Otherwise, a legal issue could arise that brings harm to both you and your client.

> Always plan to spend time building rapport during the informed consent discussion.

2

Legal and Ethical Issues

In this chapter, I will address some of the most significant ethical and legal issues that are commonly a part of a clinician's practice. Privacy and security are first and foremost on our minds when we consider the use of technology to deliver services. For you to understand what you need to ensure your client's PHI is secure, it is necessary to address HIPAA compliance and safeguards. Once you understand what vulnerabilities you have after a risk assessment, you need to put safeguards in place for the protection of the PHI. Then you can determine what risk management strategies you need to implement to protect any vulnerable areas.

After I discuss how you can address these privacy and security issues, I will look at the laws regarding interjurisdictional practice and licensing concerns. I will also discuss laws concerning informed consent, mandated reporting, and duty to warn and protect, and I will provide guidance regarding how to locate the different state laws.

Case Study
USING TELEHEALTH BEYOND QUARANTINE

Anne recently started using video sessions with her existing clients due to the stay-at-home orders during the COVID-19 pandemic. Six other mental health professionals work in her agency, and most of them decided to do the same when their business closed for in-person visits. During this emergency situation, she and her colleagues used Facetime and the free version of Skype to conduct video sessions.

After two months, the stay-at-home order was lifted, and Anne was able to open her office to conduct in-person sessions. However, many of her clients found the video sessions to be helpful and have now expressed a preference for video sessions due to the convenience of not having to leave their homes. Given that Anne lives in Illinois—where the weather sometimes keeps clients from attending scheduled sessions—she is now resolved to use TMH because she sees it as a solution to that problem, as well as other problems. Today, Anne received a phone call from a former client, Martin, who wants his first video session.

Questions to consider:

What does Anne need to do first?

_____

_____

What legal concerns are there?

_____

_____

What safeguards does she need to put in place?

_____

_____

HIPAA Compliance and Safeguards

To know the vulnerabilities that need safeguarding, HIPAA requires each clinician or agency to conduct a risk assessment to determine vulnerabilities. To assist with this, I have included the following website, which gives complete instructions on how to assess the vulnerabilities and document them: https://www.healthit.gov/topic/privacy-security-and-hipaa/security-risk-assessment-tool.

This website provides a free security risk assessment (SRA) tool and includes extensive explanations on how to use it. There is even a YouTube video on how to complete the SRA. You can download and install the SRA on any Microsoft Windows operating machine, and it is a recommended best practice. Using the SRA can aid in the security assessment process, but it is not everything you need to comply with HIPAA.

The goal of this tool is to assist clinicians in meeting the requirement of completing a risk assessment and maintaining the security of all electronic PHI, or ePHI. Each agency or clinician will find different vulnerabilities when completing the assessment. Any vulnerabilities that do not show up when completing the tool need to be documented somewhere within the tool.

Once you have documented these security risks on the SRA, you rate each area of vulnerability, and the SRA gives information on how to make improvements in each area. You need to complete the SRA annually or earlier if there are changes to assets and vendors, such as adding TMH to a practice. Once you have completed this mandatory risk assessment, it is time to determine how you will manage the risks. This is called the risk management plan. I provide more information on the SRA and the risk management plan in the next section.

Returning to the case study about Anne, it is important that she set up training for everyone in the agency to ensure they understand HIPAA mandates and to establish their understanding of the agency's policies and procedures for using telehealth. This process would look different for clinicians working alone, as policies and procedures differ when there is only one clinician as opposed to six or more. Similarly, policies and procedures would again be different if Anne was a supervisor of mental health staff at a hospital. This is one reason why a risk assessment is essential. It answers the question of what is needed for a safe practice using technology.

The HIPAA risk assessment should be an ongoing process. It is necessary to set up regular times for reviews to track access to PHI and to detect any security incidents. It is also necessary to consistently review the effectiveness of the security measures that are put in place. HHS includes the following requirements in a risk assessment. This is not an exhaustive list of what you need to include in a risk assessment, but it guides you in beginning the process:

- Evaluate the possibility of a potential risk to ePHI.

- Estimate the impact of potential risks to ePHI.

- Address the risks with appropriate security measures.

- Document the security measures and the rationale for the measures.

- Maintain consistent protections to security.

The risk assessment is crucial to the protection of ePHI because the HIPAA Security Rule states that covered entities (CEs) must ensure that all ePHI created, received, or maintained is protected. The first task may be to track where you are storing ePHI. For example, Anne has decided to store all ePHI in a cloud, and she may choose to store ePHI on databases. Now that she has determined to store the information on a cloud, there are questions to answer.

Questions to consider:

Is the cloud encrypted with HIPAA-compliant encryption?

_____

_____

What devices need to be password protected?

_____

_____

Who is authorized to access the information on the devices and databases?

_____

_____

What is the nature of the information involved?

_____

_____

What needs to be done to ensure the security of the ePHI?

_____

_____

Another reason to continue assessing security vulnerabilities is that technology is always evolving. As time goes on, new systems will be exchanged for old ones to keep pace with the times. Remember the old MS-DOS computers? That is the computer I used to obtain my bachelor's degree. That computer would not be a good choice to use in today's world. Imagine if I had resisted changing or upgrading to a new computer system because I was uncomfortable with learning a new system. I would have had to eliminate many opportunities to be of service to my clients. My old MS-DOS computer was not even connected to the internet. Even if it was connected, it did not have color—plus the screen was so small that a clear picture of the client would be impossible.

During the COVID-19 pandemic, I realized that being familiar with technology gave me options to assist my existing clients and to continue working with them. There was no break in service because that was the normal way I had been seeing them in the first place. If I had not been familiar with the use of technology to provide mental health services, then I would have only been able to provide treatment for clients via phone since I was unable to see anyone in person. However, many of my friends and colleagues had not yet decided they wanted to use video sessions, so they needed guidance.

Keeping up with changes in technology and assessing for vulnerabilities on a regular basis is part of the choice to use technology in our profession. If you read the code of ethics, it states that we are required to keep up with the current literature on technology, and I believe the importance of doing so has never been clearer than during this pandemic. Therefore, keep up with the literature and regularly assess for vulnerabilities. Consider it a regular ongoing activity.

> Keeping up on the literature behind telemental health protects you from vulnerabilities within your practice.

Let's look how keeping up to date applies to Anne's situation. Some of Anne's clients want to use secure messaging, but her mobile device is not included in the original risk assessment analysis. This means Anne needs to update the assessment and add in policies and procedures to cover the addition of secure messaging. Anne will also need to follow up to ensure all those involved are following the guidelines set in the policies and procedures. For more information on guidelines, see the resource section of this guidebook.

There are numerous agencies that have already made risk assessment their specialty, and they share tools to help you and other CEs conduct HIPAA risk assessments. At the most basic level, you need to understand where ePHI is stored, who can access it, how ePHI is viewed and used, and how risk is handled, including with business associates and vendors. I suggest that you take the time needed to develop and implement security measures that apply to your daily operations and to make sure you are meeting state and federal requirements. This will reduce the chances of experiencing a security breach.

When looking at the safeguards you need to implement, it is important to understand if the safeguard is required or addressable. Required means you must implement it, whereas addressable means you must assess whether the safeguard is reasonable and appropriate. For example, encryption is addressable, so if you address the issue but do not implement it, then you must provide thorough documentation expressing the rationale for not implementing encryption. Just because HIPAA says it is addressable does *not* mean it should not happen.

In summary, the goal of assessment is to identify potential vulnerabilities and assess the degree of the vulnerability to a threat so, ultimately, countermeasures can be put in place to reduce the known vulnerabilities. Examples of these vulnerabilities could be as simple as a weak door lock or poor passwords, or it could possibly involve a staff member who does not have the appropriate training to treat specific clients. These vulnerabilities all represent security risks that can be minimized with security measures.

CEs must understand what it means to continue setting up a safe practice with risk management, as well as what they need to do so. HIPAA requires that CEs have three types of safeguards in place: administrative, technical, and physical. These safeguards are policies and procedures that are set up to protect against breaches of PHI. Not only are these safeguards a federal requirement, but they also play an important role in ensuring that sensitive health data remains secure and out of the reach of unauthorized individuals. Each organization must review their own policies, daily workflow, and security needs to ensure the right measures are in place.

Administrative safeguards are a subset of the HIPAA Security Rule that focus on internal organization, policies, procedures, and maintenance of security measures that protect patient health information. Administrative safeguards cover areas like security management, assigned security responsibility, workforce security, information access management, security awareness and training, security incident procedures, contingency plans, evaluation, and business associate contracts and other agreements.

Technical safeguards include mechanisms that can be configured to automatically help secure your data. According to HHS, the following are necessary controls for HIPAA compliance:

- Access control

- Audit controls

- Integrity

- Person or entity authentication

- Transmission security

In Anne's situation, in order to comply with HIPAA technical safeguards, she must configure a network authentication system so each person has their own password to enter the system. One way to ensure that an effective safeguard is in place is to require everyone to have a password with uppercase and lowercase letters, as well as numbers and a symbol. Anne could also require everyone to change their password every ninety days. This would be an added safeguard.

Other technical controls include firewall settings, role-based group policy settings, the algorithm chosen to encrypt data, and a notification service that sends an email when your website identifies a failed login attempt. When it comes to passwords, the policies and procedures concerning passwords are considered an administrative safeguard, whereas the actual setting up of the network authentication system is the technical safeguard. The location and secure placement of the systems are considered physical safeguards.

Physical safeguards are the security controls in place to guard the physical aspects of securing PHI in facilities and on devices. Physical safeguards are designed to prevent unauthorized users from taking your computers or server or from plugging a USB cable directly into your Wi-Fi router. HHS has identified the following physical controls as necessary for HIPAA compliance:

- Facility access

- Workstation use

- Workstation security

- Device and media controls

For example, Anne set her clinic up so all members of her staff could have access to ePHI from workstations located in high-traffic areas. To comply with HIPAA standards, she installed screen barriers and used locking cables to make sure computers were anchored to the wall. She also stored client paperwork in a locked filing cabinet, which was located inside a locked closet with a key available only to those authorized to have it. Anne also took extra precautions and installed security cameras at the facility entrance, at exits, and in all areas where ePHI was stored. When compiling her risk management manual, she added policies and procedures for all these safeguards.

As a mental health provider, it is equally important to set up administrative, technical, and physical safeguards so you can have the best security for ePHI. Failing to maintain adequate safeguards for security in these areas could lead to fines and legal issues. It is important to invest the time needed to set up the equipment properly, write the policies and procedures, and train staff on all the aspects of privacy and security. It is all time well spent. Your organization's risk management is a protective factor for both you and your clients. Understanding risk management is essential.

Risk Management

Clinical risk management improves the quality and safety of your services because when you complete your risk analysis and assessment, you will have identified the weaknesses within your practice that put clients at risk of harm. Once you have identified these vulnerabilities, the next step is to implement safeguards to prevent or control the risks found. The best way to go about this is to hire a consultant to walk you through all the steps, starting with the risk analysis that identifies your vulnerabilities.

Because it is difficult to know everything you need to know about technology, hiring a specialist to guide you through the entire process can save time and make the process less difficult. The professional you choose to assist with your risk management should be familiar with the type of business that you run, whether you are a solo practitioner or you work for a larger agency. The goal is to reduce your security risks to reasonable and appropriate levels. Keep in mind that even when you hire a consultant, you are still responsible for ensuring that the plan has integrity by following up and ensuring staff members are trained and are implementing all the policies and procedures.

Your risk management program should contain certain elements. The first key element is to understand that the organization is best served by assigning an individual to take on the job responsibilities of a risk manager. In the case study with Anne, she has six other clinicians working with her. It could be helpful for her to assign or hire a mental health professional to take on the role of risk manager and be responsible for handling the security of all PHI. This person would have the authority to carry out the various aspects of the risk management program and have a clearly defined role. However, if you are a solo practitioner, the authority belongs to you unless you hire a consultant or choose to purchase risk management software that monitors your risk management on a regular basis.

When choosing who will take on this important position in your organization, it is a best practice to select someone who is accessible so it is easier for those involved in a breach to approach that person when there is possible risk to be reported. A possible breach or security issue can be a difficult time for a clinician, so the chosen person needs to be emotionally strong and knowledgeable in the field of risk management and security.

Before hiring a risk manager, decide the scope of the risk management program, the services provided, and the objective of the program. One objective of the program is to identify and analyze risk, as well as to implement a process to manage any identified risks. To maintain appropriate measures of risk management, an objective is to monitor the effectiveness of the risk management program on an ongoing basis. Once you have established the program's objectives, you must develop clear objectives as to what the assigned security person's job duties will be.

For example, the assigned or hired security person will develop and manage a systematic process of identifying threats through assessment, identifying the level of the threat, and correcting threats. This person will also act as a liaison with all involved in the risk management process by serving as the first point of contact when there is a breach and by speaking or writing to all those who need to be contacted after a breach. Part of this systematic process includes developing a protocol of what to do when a breach is discovered.

The first step in this protocol might be to immediately report the breach to one's supervisor in writing, as well as to the assigned risk manager. Once a potential breach is reported, the assigned security person completes an assessment of harm to determine the necessary next steps to protect those involved. It is important to decide on a policy that determines how to protect and preserve evidence of the possible breach for a later claims investigation. The security person will develop a strategy to protect the organization, the clinician, and the client, and they will also access legal counsel. This person must be assertive and able to withstand interrogations if needed and be supportive to staff. Of course, there are more steps in this protocol, so be sure your assigned person, consultant, or purchased software is complete to manage your organizational needs.

When it comes to risk management, you must determine and adhere to your organization's policies and procedures. A policy is a predetermined course of action established as a guide, and it reflects the objectives of the organization. A policy is a document that outlines what everyone in the organization must do or not do, and it gives directions, limits, and decision-making guidance. In contrast, a procedure is the means or steps by which a policy's actions can be accomplished. Procedures determine in a concrete way how all major decisions, activities, and actions will take place within the boundaries that are set by the policies. Once an organization's policies and procedures are written, there is no searching or questioning how to adhere to its policies. Policies are considered the law of the organization, and they minimize risks when adhered to.

For Anne to ensure she has a safe and secure TMH practice, she needs to write policies and procedures, and she needs to define the structure by which she will implement them with her program. These policies and procedures will minimize potential errors and risks and, in the long run, could save her from ethical or legal battles. The following section describes some of the necessary policies and procedures for Anne to include.

Policies and Procedures

Scope of practice: Here Anne will include the services that she and her staff are permitted to legally provide. She wants to be certain her staff only practice within their scope of practice. When a licensed professional practices outside the scope of their practice, it could result in a sanction to the institution or a personal sanction by the licensing board, along with limits placed on the ability to practice. The worst-case scenario is that a provider's license could be removed. Therefore, Anne is making sure this section is included in her risk management policies and procedures. She also wants her staff to practice TMH based on their education, experiences, and competence. Therefore, she will implement a policy and procedure that requires each staff member to have an active license. She will also require that all staff members complete continuing education requirements as recommended by the licensing board. To ensure the integrity of the policy, she will develop predetermined consequences should a staff member fail to maintain an active license.

Staff training and orientation: Anne has also decided she wants to include a specified time limit on following through with obtaining licensure and education. This includes initial training on the risk management program and HIPAA safety training and updates. For instance, she might write a safeguard to indicate that when a new person starts, they have two weeks to complete training on the agency's risk management program. She might also decide that providers who fail to adhere to this policy will be given notice about the amount of time they have to complete the training, or they will be terminated from employment. It is important to include the consequences should providers not complete the tasks within the given time frame. This adds integrity to the program and shows how compliance is maintained.

Standard of care: Anne wants to include in her policies what she considers to be a reasonable appropriate degree of attention and caution in providing services, as well as the consequences that arise if a provider does not adhere to this standard of care. For example, she could develop policies and procedures on establishing and maintaining an ongoing and updated treatment plan for each client.

Questions to consider:

How can Anne handle the provision of treatment plans in a safe and secure way?

_____

_____

When should Anne require providers to complete a treatment plan by?

_____

_____

What are some consequences Anne might enact if providers do not adhere to this policy and procedure?

_____

_____

Services offered: Here is where Anne will include the services her staff will offer based on appropriate licensing requirements, education, and training in the use of technology.

Use of technology: The policies and procedures here will outline how to use technology in a safe and secure way and who has access to each device. This may also include the circumstances under which technology is used and the result should the policies be ignored.

Confidentiality and privacy: In this section, Anne will include instructions on how the staff will maintain client confidentiality, privacy, and security. She may include confidentiality statements for staff to sign, instructions on how to safely secure and store PHI, guidelines regarding the use or non-use of mobile phones, and printing policies and procedures.

Record keeping: This area will include information on what records are kept, how long records will be kept, and how they will be kept. This policy may also describe how Anne will protect records from loss, damage, or alteration. However, it is always best practice to follow the law on employee record keeping. Check your state laws when writing this policy. For example, in Illinois, employee records must be kept for six years. In addition, Illinois states that employers with over fifteen employees are subject to record-keeping laws.

Documentation: Anne needs to develop policies and procedures to ensure staff members maintain proper documentation that supports quality client care regarding treatment, continuity of care, and accurate and timely claims for payment. Anne needs to include guidance as part of this policy, along with procedures that support the integrity of the PHI. For instance, she should include guidelines about having a record for all clients, documenting entries in a timely manner, the use of abbreviations and symbols, how to make corrections, the use of appropriate words and phrasing, and the format to use when documenting. She also needs to include policies that describe how to protect client information when obtaining payments or requesting payments. Procedures could be as simple as identifying a late entry and how to document an omission.

Usage of platform: Anne could include numerous policies in this section, and the accompanying procedures may be extensive. The policies need to cover the use of platforms and the rules that are established concerning their use.

Recording sessions: Anne needs to include a policy on whether recording sessions is permitted, including the circumstances under which recording is permitted, how it needs to happen, how the security is set up, and what happens when providers do not adhere to this policy.

Telephone calls: Policies and procedures here would describe what telephones are permitted for business use versus personal use. This would also include other policies concerning privacy and security, and how that needs to be accomplished, and the protocol when policies and procedures are ignored.

Text messaging: Anne also needs policies and procedures regarding the use of instant messages and text messages, including the types of devices that are permitted for messaging, the types of messages that are allowed, the security measures in place for messaging (such as encryption), and the storage of these messages.

Emails: These policies and procedures may be somewhat like those regarding text messaging. Anne would want to address the type of email account that is acceptable for business communications and whether it is acceptable to transmit all types of data over this email system. In addition, she would want to consider whether providers can use business emails for personal messages and the consequences of not adhering to these policies and procedures.

Videoconferencing: Here is where Anne would write policies and procedures to determine what devices are permitted for video conferencing, how these devices are used and set up for security and privacy, how these devices are maintained and updated, and the consequences if protocols are not followed.

Social media: The policies and procedures for the use of social media will differ depending on the services offered by each agency or with each clinician. For example, my social media policy is that I do not interact with clients or former clients on social media of any kind. Others have told me that they use social media to obtain clients. This could be a large or small section depending on your practices.

Reimbursement: These policies and procedures would describe the issue of collections and payments, and how to obtain and receive them in a safe manner. In addition, it would describe when a clinician would enlist assistance from a third party for collection, including how to do so both legally and ethically. These policies and procedures will differ across clinicians based on their practices and preferences.

Entire manuals have been written on the topic of risk management, and choosing the one that assists you in this process can be intimidating. In writing this book, it is my intention to guide you in understanding the need for risk assessment and management. I also want to help you understand some of the topics that you need to include within your risk management plan and to show you where to get additional guidance to complete your risk management program.

To complete this section, I have included some questions to consider that will help you get started with your risk management plan. After that, I have included a copy of a sample policy and procedure document. Be sure to seek consultation based on your organizational needs and your financial situation, and then take the time to document all communications throughout the process. The depth of your risk management needs depends on so many things, such as the size of your organization and the elements of your practice. There is no one-size-fits-all approach in risk management. Connect with someone for assistance, even if you are a solo practitioner. Peace of mind has unending worth.

Questions to consider:

Who has authority and responsibility for each security consideration?

_____

_____

What is the scope of a risk management plan?

_____

_____

What are the objectives of a risk management plan?

_____

_____

What are the processes for risk identification, analysis, and control?

_____

_____

How will information concerning risk management be distributed?

_____

_____

What important policies and procedures are necessary?

_____

_____

Protect your clients, your organization, and your peace of mind by ensuring that every telemental health service you provide has a place in your risk management plan.

Sample Policy and Procedure

ABC Counseling Services
Policy # 002
Title: Plan for Professional Services
Effective Date: 5/1/2020   Authorized By: Marie Copes, Owner of ABC

Policy: It is the policy of ABC Counseling Services to maintain a Plan for Professional Services, including staff composition and service descriptions.

Procedure:
1. The Plan for Professional services shall be a comprehensive description of the organization and services in total.
2. The Plan for Professional Services is reviewed annually, revised as necessary, and approved by the owner of ABC.
3. The Plan for Professional Services shall include, but is not limited to, all the following:
   a. Introduction
   b. Purpose, goals, and objectives
   c. Mission statement and philosophy
   d. Needs assessment
   e. Population serviced, including special populations
   f. Program goals
   g. Description of services
   h. Hours of operation and after-hours contact information
   i. Service goals and objectives
   j. Operational objectives
   k. Organizational resources to meet client needs
   l. General admission criteria
   m. Screening/intake/assessment process
   n. Treatment planning process
   o. Treatment planning
   p. Treatment modalities
   q. Proper utilization of program
   r. Waiting list management
   s. Affiliate resources

The Plan for Professional Services shall be accessible to all employees, clients, consumer groups, and funding sources, as well as to the licensing or accrediting body.

Payment Compliance

Maintaining HIPAA and payment card industry (PCI) compliance is needed to protect and secure any information sent using technology for payment. Your payment processing and financial transaction must be HIPAA compliant and meet PCI standards. HIPAA compliance audits are required by federal law and are based on the HHS Office of Civil Rights protocols. HIPAA and PCI have different audit guidelines, safeguard requirements, and consequences for non-compliance. HIPAA guidelines are focused on policies, training, and processes, and failure to meet HIPAA compliance guidelines can result in fines and jail time.

Case Study

PAYMENT OPTIONS WITH TELEHEALTH

Joe presents for treatment five years after a history of in-person treatment for depression, which began when he was processing his divorce from his wife. He now wants to return to treatment to work through some relationship concerns. He agrees that video sessions will be helpful since he works at home, but he is concerned about how he will pay for sessions.

Questions to consider:

What options are there to collect payment from Joe?

_____

_____

What policies and procedures are there concerning collection?

_____

_____

HIPAA involves protecting a client's health information contained in electronic health records (EHR) or electronic medical records (EMR), while PCI involves payment processing. Payment information is part of PHI and is subject to HIPAA compliance. Although HIPAA allows CEs to disclose payment information to third parties for the purpose of collecting monies owed for services offered, this does not excuse providers from protecting the information shared. Failure to comply with PCI guidelines is not a criminal offense, but non-compliance can result in large fines and the loss of credit card processing privileges.

When collecting payments, there are some best practices to incorporate. The first is to ask your credit card platform to sign a business associate agreement (BAA). Platforms that are set up for telehealth usually offer one. The concern is to ensure that you have signed it and that you have set up your technology appropriately. Having a formal consultation with a technology expert will give you answers on setting up your computer or device in the safest way.

Another best practice is to ensure that you are using at least a two-factor authentication for the collection of payments when working from home. This could include having a code sent to your phone or computer that you need to input when collecting payments for treatment. In addition, establish policies that prohibit clinicians from saving any files on their home computers or from printing client information at home on their personal printers, unless their location at home is set up with technical and physical safeguards to ensure privacy and confidentiality.

It is also a best practice to avoid storing unencrypted payment card information. If you must store payment card information, be sure to encrypt the information and set up the necessary safeguards to protect that information. A CE might consider a software platform that processes the payments by not storing any information.

Another best practice is to use terminals that support Europay, MasterCard, and Visa (EMV) chip technology for payments or sales. These credit cards contain a computer chip that users insert into a device as opposed to swiping it. According to Visa, in-store credit fraud dropped 70 percent when merchants began to accept EMV.

Another standard in payment data security is PCI-validated point-to-point encryption (vP2PE), which requires all data to be encrypted immediately upon receiving it. This is a best practice since the data is immediately encrypted while it travels through the servers, and the client's card number is therefore encrypted and undecipherable.

A HIPAA-compliant platform that offers safe billing is a good choice for payment collections. If you consider Joe from the earlier case scenario, he might be relieved to know that your chosen platform does not store his payment information and that it processes collections in compliance with national standards. With your platform, the work to secure the client's PHI has already been done. As the clinician, your responsibility is to make sure your safeguards are in place and that your client is informed of his responsibilities to safeguard his information on his end.

When presenting on the laws and ethics of using technology, I have received many questions on what to use for collecting payments. Many who attend my seminars are in private practice and do not have budgets to hire specialists or set up expensive software. The bottom line is that you will need to have a BAA with your chosen processor, and you will then need to do your part to set up safeguards to ensure that you are fully HIPAA compliant. Here is some additional guidance to help you stay HIPAA compliant.

The first thing you want to do is to find a processor that will sign a BAA. There is an exception to the BAA rule with HIPAA that says if your credit card processor only provides credit card processing and nothing else, then you may not need a BAA.

When accepting credit card payments, make sure your processor does not send credit card receipts through SMS messages. Options such as Square send electronic receipts to clients through text messages, and this is a HIPAA violation because this information is PHI. You can take care of this issue by sending clients receipts in the mail or through a secure messaging system. Square is now offering a BAA, but you as the clinician are still responsible for your part in setting things up in compliance. A best practice is to choose a processor from whom you can obtain a BAA, but that is just the beginning. Be sure to do your part by putting in place the safeguards I discussed earlier.

When storing credit card numbers, be sure to secure them under lock and key with no unauthorized access. This is true of the security of your swiping hardware too. Since you may be taking this information over the internet, you also need to use a secure terminal and ensure that the communication concerning payment is secure. Again, I always suggest using a HIPAA-compliant platform with a BAA and secure payment options.

Following these guidelines keeps you and your clients safer than if you are not compliant. This is how you can protect the payment communication, protect the hardware, and ultimately protect your client from breaches of their information. For more information on how to take credit card payments and follow the national guidelines, here is a website that includes a manual on compliance: https://www.pcicomplianceguide.org/faq/. Be sure to get comfortable before starting this reading.

State Licensing Laws

Most jurisdictions have state boards that provide the necessary expertise for public protection through the regulation of the practice of mental health. Most of these boards have board members who determine what constitutes practice within the scope of the license. Because the scope of practice changes as the practice evolves, boards may need to determine the appropriateness of mental health sessions as they relate to both the established and evolving scope of practice. This is especially true with the use of technology for mental health treatment.

Five years ago, many providers who attended my seminars about technology did not use video sessions. They attended my seminar to learn about technology and to help them decide about whether they wanted to begin using technology options to serve their clients. However, today things are much different, and most providers have been forced to consider the use of video conferencing as an option due to social distancing requirements and stay-at-home orders all over our nation. This has left many unanswered questions about TMH concerning the laws and rules for clinicians.

Even though technology makes it easy for clinicians to treat clients all over the world, there are laws and rules about this for public protection. The most important thing to understand is that when a clinician is licensed and physically located in a state different from their client, both states have jurisdiction. Therefore, the practicing clinician must understand the laws in both states to provide treatment.

Interjurisdictional Laws

Some states allow clinicians to see clients in that state if the clinician holds a license in another state, but other states do not allow this. Since it is impossible to learn everything within the law in every state, I have found that it is more helpful to know where to find this information when you need it. Lawyers and mental health professionals have completed the work for us by compiling fifty state reviews of the laws concerning practice in the different states. Websites with these fifty state reviews are in the resource section of this book. When you go to those websites, you can click on the state and obtain information concerning that state's laws in most health practices. All you must do is put the web address in your search field and push enter. You will then be taken to the website to begin the process of looking for the information you need.

Case Study

CROSSING STATE LINES

Shane is a 38-year-old single man who has been seeing Sarah for six months for extreme anxiety and grief over losing his brother in a car accident. Shane is making progress in processing through his grief, but his anxiety is still causing him problems. He refuses to see a doctor, stating that he is in great health and does not want to take medication for anxiety. Shane is applying some of the new techniques for handling his anxiety and feels good about his progress.

One day, Shane comes in for a session and informs Sarah that his job is sending him to California for a one-month assignment. He knows Sarah added video sessions as another option for clients to receive treatment, so he wants to set up video sessions with her before he leaves. He is afraid he will have anxiety over the distance assignment, which might keep him from succeeding. His assignment begins in two weeks, and Sarah wants to help him, but she is not licensed in California.

Questions to consider:

What can Sarah do in this situation?

_____

_____

What legal and ethical concerns does she need to address?

_____

_____

What does Sarah need to do to have video sessions with Shane?

_____

_____

Some states have temporary practice provisions that permit clinicians to see clients for a short period of time if the clinician meets certain criteria. Clinicians can find state provisions by searching within the general rules of the telehealth laws of the licensing board. In the resource section of this book, you will find the websites I refer to in this section. When you go to one of the websites, find the state you are interested in searching, and then find your profession within that state's entry. After that, you can search for the section that gives you information on temporary practice rules. The site will usually provide you with a link that takes you directly to the board that published the rules, and you can search there to find the latest information.

When you contact the board to ask questions, be sure to document the conversation and the results. Sending emails to the board and receiving advice in concrete written form is always better than a phone conversation, so I prefer email and written answers I can document. When I am unable to get answers, I contact a mental health attorney for legal guidance, and I document that communication in the client's file.

Mental health professionals repeatedly ask if it is legal to practice across state lines or in other countries. The answer is not a simple one, and it is changing constantly in our ever-changing world. Previously, to practice across state lines, it depended on whether a clinician was licensed in the state where the client resided. Practicing across state lines is generally determined by the laws in the state of license and the laws in the state where the client is located. Once a licensed professional obtains a state license, it becomes possible to apply to the licensing board in another state. However, each state board has rules about receiving licenses from other states.

Presently, some states are working to make it easier for established professionals to practice legally in their state. The state boards for physicians and nurses have managed to gain a lot of legal and ethical support to make it easier for these professionals to practice in more than one state with only one license. Yet, for mental health professionals, it remains a task. Since all states are not the same, it is important that you consider the laws of that state and the rules of the boards. Your licensing board determines whether you keep your license, so be sure to follow those rules. If they are stricter than the state rules, follow the strictest to be safe.

When we consider the case study involving Sarah and Shane, there are several things Sarah could do. First, she could attempt to work with Shane in the session and teach him coping skills he can use to address the concerns he has while he is gone. This way, he could possibly be empowered to handle things independently. After all, we do not want to encourage dependence in our relationships with our clients. This is a good opportunity for Shane to try out his new skills for a longer period.

Since we are discussing interjurisdictional concerns here, we know that Sarah does not have time to get a California license in time to legally have a session with Shane while he is away. However, she could search to see if California allows clinicians to obtain a temporary license or if there is a temporary provision allowing clinicians to see clients on a short-term basis from another state. If she finds that this is possible, she would need to check what the requirements are to temporarily practice in California. Then she would need to check with her licensing board to make sure she is legally allowed to practice in another state with her license. Even though California may say she can see Shane while he is in California, Sarah's state licensing board may say that is not legal.

There are movements that are making it easier to practice across state lines. One of those is called the Psychology Interjurisdictional Compact (PSYPACT), which is for psychologists. The PSYPACT involves an interstate compact that was put into place to facilitate the practice of telepsychology across state lines and the temporary in-person, face-to-face practice of psychology across state lines for up to thirty days. According to the PSYPACT website, at the time of writing this guidebook, approximately twelve states have enacted the PSYPACT legislation, and seventeen are pending. This number is changing regularly due to the evolving nature of the COVID-19 pandemic, so it is important to check the website for the latest information and the most current updates on which states are part of PSYPACT. The website is in the resource section of this guidebook.

Another program that was introduced for practicing across state lines is the Anywhere to Anywhere program. This program is a federal initiative that applies to telemedicine services that veterans access online through a website or through VA Video Connect. VA Video Connect is a telemedicine app that the Veterans Administration (VA) began using in 2017. This app allows veterans to schedule appointments and have contact with their clinician from anywhere. Clients can schedule a video session with their provider, and they can also include their family in the session. At the time of this writing, the VA was working diligently to upgrade the services available on this app.

The Anywhere to Anywhere Program allows the VA to provide health services, including mental health services, to veterans across state lines. This program expands the opportunities for clinicians to offer telehealth to veterans and their families. It makes it easier for those living in rural areas, where no treatment centers are nearby, to access clinicians. When veterans are involved in treatment and must relocate to another state, they can continue treatment with the same provider. In addition, when veterans need specialized mental health care, there is a much better chance they will find the right clinician with the state boundaries being removed.

While I presented a seminar at Fort Pendleton, California, the mental health professionals shared with me that most of them were not licensed in California, yet they were able to provide mental health treatment to the military on base through the VA because of the Anywhere to Anywhere program. Some participants shared with me that there were problems with the technology at times, but not many problems with the licensing. Although all participants in attendance carried a license from another state in the United States, many were still working on obtaining a California license. The Anywhere to Anywhere Program allows for many opportunities should a licensed professional want to provide treatment to the military and their families. It is one of the ways to legally provide treatment in other states with only one license.

Another initiative that allows professionals to have a license in one state and serve clients in another is the Indian Health Service (IHS), which is the principal federal health care provider and health advocate for American Indians and Alaskan Natives. Its mission is to raise their physical, mental, social, and spiritual health status to the highest possible level. The IHS website, which gives more information about this group and the opportunities for providers to serve this clientele, is in the resource section of this guidebook.

When I read about the Anywhere to Anywhere and IHS programs, I was encouraged that someday it will be much easier for those of us with the appropriate licensure and educational qualifications to serve populations both legally and ethically from a distance. It would be completely different if the licensing laws were to allow clinicians to see clients from anywhere as long as the clinician held a license in the state in which they were located at the time of the session. However, part of the concern is that states want to protect their residents.

For states to protect the people in their jurisdiction, licensing is mandatory and there are set educational standards in each state. Some states do not require the same level of education, and states also differ in their requirements for licensure, including differences in continuing education and testing. If you had a child seeking treatment, you would want their clinician to be properly educated and trained according to the standards proposed in your state, so when you look at interjurisdictional laws through the lens of client protection, it makes sense why it is difficult to practice across state lines or to obtain a second license.

Another reason that it is sometimes difficult to obtain a second license is that states have differing laws, such as those pertaining to mandated reporting, duty to warn, domestic violence, and other significant statutes. These are just a few reasons why some states require clinicians to take a class on the state's laws if they want to treat someone in that state. In Florida, you are required to take a class on their laws regarding domestic violence, HIV, medical errors, and a few other topics. In some states, you are not required to take any of those classes.

Questions to consider:

In what states do you want to obtain a license?

_____

_____

What steps do you need to take to accomplish this?

_____

_____

According to the website for the Association of State and Provincial Psychology Boards (ASPPB), there are four steps to follow if you want to practice telepsychology under the authority of PSYPACT. First, you need to apply for and obtain an E.Passport from the ASPPB. Second, you must apply for and obtain an Authority to Practice Interjurisdictional Telepsychology (APIT) from the PSYPACT Commission. After you receive the approvals, you may begin practicing telepsychology, but you must update your home state and abide by the scope of practice in the receiving state. The home state is where you are located at the time of services, and the receiving state is where the client is at the time of provision. Lastly, to maintain the E.Passport, you will need to complete, on an annual basis, the required three credit hours relevant to the use of technology in psychology.

Case Study
ANOTHER STATE LINE CONUNDRUM

Mark, a social worker with a clinical private practice in Missouri, is seeing James using video sessions. He has seen James for six sessions, and they have built good rapport, so James is comfortable sharing his concerns with Mark. Today, James shares that he believes he is addicted to gaming with his friends, and he thinks it is ruining his marriage. He also shares that his wife wants him to move to Texas, so they are moving in three weeks. James wants to continue treatment with Mark even though he will be in Texas and refuses to see someone else in Texas. He explains that he does not want his in-laws to know he is involved in treatment.

Questions to consider:

How can Mark legally treat James in another state?

_____

_____

What are the ethical considerations in this case?

_____

_____

The first thing Mark may want to do is check with his licensing board to see if he is legally allowed to see someone in Texas. If his licensing state board gives him a green light, then he will have to check with the Texas state board to ensure they approve of him seeing someone in Texas. If Texas tells him he can see a client that is in Texas, James will need to become familiar with the relevant laws and regulatory requirements in Texas, such as laws concerning informed consent, mandated reporting, and duty to warn or protect. If James were a teen, he would also need to know laws on age of consent and other legislation. Mark will also need to check with his liability insurance to see if he is covered when he sees James in another state where he is not licensed.

James pays through his insurance company, so Mark will also need to inquire whether they will cover the sessions when James is in another state. Each step of this process requires documentation. Documenting the rationale for using technology with this client may include continuity of care in the best interest of the client.

Case Study
HOW MUCH IS TOO MUCH?

Mark is seeing another client, Diane, for the treatment of trauma and panic attacks, which she experiences due to a relationship that ended after repeated domestic violence. She is a long-term client of six months and is finally starting to gain confidence. She is going on vacation for two weeks and does not want to stop sessions during this time. She is concerned she will have a panic attack while she is away and be unable to cope. She does not know if she can survive without Mark's support and wants to know if she can call him should she need his help. Diane is showing signs of dependency.

Although we can be thankful that Diane wants to get help for her concerns, there are some things Mark can do to equip her before she goes on vacation. He can research the local resources in the area in which she is vacationing. This could give her confidence that there are others who can help her should the need arise. He can also role-play with her and equip her with coping skills to sustain her through a panic attack. It also makes sense for him to review with her their agreement regarding informed consent and the handling of emergencies. Clinicians should always determine and discuss information regarding emergencies at the initial visit when the informed consent is reviewed. Informed consent is an ongoing process; it is not a one-time event.

Informed Consent

Informed consent gives clients the ability to make informed decisions about participating or not participating in treatment. By law and according to ethics, clients have a right to understand what the risks and benefits are of the treatment in which they are participating. Clients also have a right to know the details of participation, such as privacy and confidentiality, costs, reasons for termination, cancellation policies, and other issues, which I will discuss in this section.

When our practices strictly involved in-person sessions, we completed informed consent in the office and discussed it with the client during our first session. Now that we have added technology as a method of delivering services, informed consent takes on new considerations. It is now important for clinicians to know what the laws are in the state where the client is at the time of the session, as well as the laws where the clinician is located, and to follow both sets of laws. Most states will require that clinicians obtain informed consent before providing services. When conducting TMH, some states require that you complete informed consent with both audio and visual in real time, and some say only real time is necessary. Therefore, you must check the laws in the state where you are *and* where the client is at the time of the sessions.

Clinicians also need a safe procedure for delivering and receiving forms to clients. An ethical standard is for clinicians to conduct a discussion to ensure clients understand and know what they are consenting to. This communication should be documented in the client's file. Some research has found that using a modified informed consent form (e.g., one that provides images and bullet points for clients to sign and agree to) is more effective in allowing the client to more easily understand its content (Duvall Antonacopoulos & Serin, 2016). Therefore, reviewing a checklist of the main points with clients can assist in helping them become more informed. This can be accomplished using an online format combined with real-time communication.

In my practice, I have developed a checklist of the important information I need to review in an informed consent document, and I then review this with my client prior to beginning treatment. I then document in my files that I have reviewed this checklist of information and that, at the time of the discussion, the client stated and appeared to understand the consent given to proceed. Once the informed consent forms are completed, it is a good practice to consult with experts or someone with many years of practice and document the conversation.

Let's consider the case scenario with Diane and Mark again. Diane has a legal and ethical right to know what the risks and benefits are of proceeding with sessions using technology. An important element of informed consent is to ensure that Diane is making this decision with full knowledge and understanding of these risks and benefits. Respecting clients' dignity and autonomy is a fundamental principle of ethical decision making. The first way Mark can maintain this standard is to ensure Diane understands what she is consenting to prior to sharing her personal health information to receive treatment. Mark can accomplish this by providing her with clear information about alternative treatments she can participate in while on vacation, as well as by reviewing the possible risks and benefits of using technology. For example, there is the benefit of sharing information with others who may be involved in her care and the possible risk of privacy being breached during the transmission of that information.

Mark must also inform Diane of the confidentiality standards and how her information will be protected, stored, and removed when legally permitted. Diane has already expressed that confidentiality is an important element in moving forward with treatment using video sessions, so reviewing this during the informed consent discussion is imperative, along with documentation of this communication. You always want clients to feel comfortable with their informed decision to proceed.

In addition to safety measures to protect Diane's information, informed consent must include reasons for ending treatment. While Diane is on vacation, she may decide she is no longer comfortable with video sessions, and she may want to be seen in person upon her return. Revisiting alternative treatments can bring about a smoother transition. Further, Diane may need a different type of treatment for several reasons, so it is important that Mark include termination in the informed consent document. Along with termination, he would want to include information on the treatment Diane is agreeing to, as well as guidelines on the number of anticipated sessions she will require to complete her treatment.

Mark can accomplish these goals when he reviews the main components of the informed consent document with Diane. As I mentioned earlier, one method that works well is to have a checklist containing the main components you need to discuss. When reviewing the informed consent form, you can check off each component when you are assured that the client has acquired understanding. After having this important informed consent discussion, it is necessary that you document the communication, including any questions the client proposed, and any concerns noted and relieved.

The next step for Mark is to send the informed consent documents to Diane in a way that protects her privacy. There are several ways this can happen:

- He can send the forms in the mail if the envelope does not disclose what is inside and who is sending the forms.

- He can send the forms via encrypted email if Diane is aware of the risks to privacy and she agrees to those risks.

- He can send the forms via a HIPAA-complaint platform with all the safeguards in place to protect the data exchange.

The laws on informed consent are different in each state, so I have provided websites that give you that information in the resources section at the end of this book. Clinicians can view current policies for all fifty states regarding client consent for TMH at the Center for Connected Health and the ATA.

In chapter 7, I provide two samples of informed consent forms for TMH to assist you in designing your own. I have also included two emergency plan forms that may provide guidance for your organization.

> Know the facts. A well-informed person is the best defense.

Mandated Reporting

The Federal Child Abuse Prevention and Treatment Act requires each state to have provisions or procedures that require certain individuals to report known or suspected instances of child abuse and neglect. HHS found that forty-eight states have mandatory reporting laws that require certain people who have frequent contact with children because of their profession to report. While it is mandatory in some jurisdictions to report suspicion of abuse and neglect—whether it is physical abuse, emotional abuse, or sexual abuse—the standards vary from state to state. It would be impossible to know all this information, and the good news is that we do not have to memorize it. A breakdown is provided, state by state, at https://www.childwelfare.gov.

On this mandated reporter website, clinicians will find information about reporting laws and requirements in each state, including Puerto Rico. The website also includes valuable information on who is a mandated reporter according to that state and what the standards are for reporting. For example, the website documents that in some states, all clinicians must report suspected child abuse or neglect, but in other states, it does not specify the professions required to report and notes that any person is permitted to report.

Duty to Warn or Protect

A duty to warn is a concept that arises in the law of torts in several circumstances, and it indicates that a party will be held liable for injuries caused to another, where the party had the opportunity to warn the other of harm and failed to do so. It is a clinician's duty to warn an identifiable potential victim of any proposed threat to harm. It is also the clinician's duty to protect clients and others from foreseeable harm by sharing confidential information with the people or organizations that can minimize or eliminate the danger.

When there is a threat of harm, it is important to conduct an assessment of the threat, including the client's past history of violent behavior, as well as their recent symptom progression. This gives you important information concerning the seriousness and specificity of the threat. Clinicians are then responsible for informing third parties if a client poses a threat to themselves or others. This is one of the HIPAA exceptions that allows a clinician to breach confidentiality for the protection of others.

When you are seeing clients in states other than your original licensed state, it is important that you understand the laws concerning this before proceeding. States differ in domestic violence laws, such as duty to warn or protect. Understanding these laws and the differences in the states where you practice is important. These laws protect clinicians from a legal battle as long as they are understood and adhered to.

There are different viewpoints concerning duty to warn and protect, especially in domestic violence situations. That could be a reason why not all states have a duty to warn statute. It is important that you follow the law of the state where your client is located and follow an ethical decision-making process when a concern arises. Although the statutes are different in many states, most require that a clear threat is voiced, that there is an identifiable victim, and that the victim is in imminent danger for the duty to warn to apply. When you are in doubt of what to do, this is a good time to consult with a supervisor, trusted colleague, or mental health attorney. Documenting all these communications is a must, along with the steps you took and the rationale for your choices.

Code of Ethics

As licensed clinicians, we are required to follow the code of ethics of our profession. Although I mention the code of ethics throughout this book, I do not mention some codes, and others are worth mentioning again. The reason this section is relevant is because ethical issues come up when using technology, and the interpretation of the code of ethics becomes a concern at times. My intention is to inspire clarity within yourself about your interpretation of these codes and to increase your understanding of the codes as they relate to your work. I will use codes from five different sources: the American Counseling Association, American Psychological Association, National Association of Social Workers, American Nurses Association, and American Mental Health Counselors Association.

Since the code of ethics is offered to guide our decision making and conduct, it is a good practice to have a decision-making model to follow. There are many published models, but for this section, I offer the model developed using Roberts's seven-stage crisis intervention model (Roberts, 2005). I have reworded some of it to make it applicable for working through dilemmas in our professions.

When there is an ethical dilemma, the first thing to do is figure out what the dilemma is. We may need to complete an assessment or simply have a session with our client to determine the problem that needs solving. Next, for our client to trust us to share information needed to solve an issue or problem, it is necessary to build rapport with them. Once we have identified the issue and built rapport, the next step is to list strategies that would solve the problem. After that, we look at the pros and cons of each plan and choose one that may best resolve the issue. Lastly, we develop a follow-up plan because we may need to go back and use other strategies to solve the problem. We also always document the entire decision-making process for future retrieval.

Case Study
VIRTUAL COUPLES THERAPY AND SOCIAL MEDIA STRIFE

A therapist named Kay has been seeing Andrew using video sessions for three months. His treatment goal is to learn new relationship skills to gain trust from his wife again. Four months ago, they separated, and his wife was referred to another therapist for individual counseling. His wife is now living in another state with her mother. After three months, Andrew is making progress in communicating with his wife, and they are beginning to talk about getting back together. Andrew wants his wife to join the sessions now. Kay wants to help Andrew and his wife continue their journey of repairing their marriage, but she is unsure how to proceed ethically. Andrew suggests using Facetime. He also wants Kay to look at his wife's Facebook account before starting sessions together. He wants Kay's opinion on things his wife has posted.

Questions to consider:

What ethical issues are present?

_____

_____

What resolutions are there to each one?

_____

_____

What steps does Kay need to take?

_____

_____

Kay has many ethical issues presented in this scenario. The issues that are relevant for Kay could differ for other clinicians, depending on their circumstances. For example, for Kay to use video sessions, the code of ethics states that she and the client must be competent to use the chosen technology. For the sake of this example, we assume this is not a problem.

Another dilemma that is evident is whether Kay can add Andrew's wife as a potential client since Kay is located in a different state. She will need to review interjurisdictional laws and consider the board's code of ethics. This could stop the process of couples counseling until Andrew and his wife move back in together. Kay also must be aware of the laws both in the state where Andrew's wife lives and where Andrew lives. Although this is not a problem when she is only seeing Andrew, adding his wife to sessions could be an issue because that would mean she is practicing in another state. In addition, Andrew's wife then becomes Kay's client when they are in sessions, so she will also need to have informed consent from her. Kay completed an informed consent form with Andrew, but if she adds his wife to the video sessions, she will need to go over this form with her as well. She can review this informed consent document with Andrew and his wife during the initial visit when they begin couples counseling.

Kay will also need to complete a form that shows she has an emergency plan for both Andrew in his state and Andrew's wife in the state where she is located. The informed consent form will include the risks and benefits of using technology, alternate methods of use if the technology fails, and response times. (See the informed consent section for more information.)

Another issue Kay is facing concerns the use of Facetime. As you recall, Facetime is not HIPAA compliant and is only permitted in emergency situations, such as the emergency state of the pandemic. At that time, permissions were given to allow clinicians to use Facetime and other mediums. But even though Facetime was allowed, HIPAA-compliant platforms were available and should always be the first choice. Kay will need to ensure her HIPAA-compliant platform works for Andrew on his device, and she will need to make sure he is educated on his responsibility for keeping the sessions private and secure.

Andrew also wants Kay to view his wife's Facebook account without her permission. This is another ethical issue that needs to be resolved. In the American Counseling Association code of ethics, counselors are to respect the privacy of their clients on social media and obtain permission before viewing a client's social media account. Kay decided she would use Andrew's request to help him become more self-aware about his issues with trusting his wife.

In a seminar I presented last year, I recall a mental health professional came up to me at break time and told me that a former client of ten years ago contacted her on Facebook and asked if she would like to go lunch and get caught up. The professional said she always thought they would be good friends in another world, and she really wanted to make this connection. She asked me what I thought. I have had clients return for treatment as much as ten years after their last session, and I am always thankful that I can continue seeing them. One of the reasons I can assist them is that I respect the code of ethics that says a client always remains a client. This code is different in other professions. Some codes say you can begin a new relationship with a past client after five years, and others give a different time frame. I have decided that for me personally, I will remain available as a clinician so as not to blur boundaries.

The code of ethics is something that you should review and refer to any time you are faced with an ethical dilemma. When this occurs, document the steps you took to resolve the issue using an ethical decision-making model. In addition, use consultation and supervision—and document these communications—to show the integrity of your choices.

Given that I refer to the code of ethics throughout this book, I will conclude this section with some advice that has always assisted me in making difficult decisions. No matter what the situation, we can always choose to do our best and hope that we inspire others to do the same. When we do not choose to follow the code of ethics, we may be faced with crossing an ethical boundary.

Boundary Issues

The code of ethics addresses many issues surrounding boundaries when using technology, which is why I have included the previous section on the code of ethics. Here I will further address some of the boundary issues that relate to a TMH practice. There are many definitions of what a boundary is, but the one I appreciate the most is from www.vocabulary.com: a boundary is a border or line drawn that can either be physical, such as a wall between two properties, or abstract, such as a moral boundary that people decide is wrong to cross. Boundaries can also be emotional, physical, or digital. When we go back and read the case study with Kay and Andrew in the previous section, there are significant issues with boundaries. Let us review!

The first boundary issue pertains to the use of Facetime to conduct a session. This violates laws since mental health professionals are not to use non-HIPAA-compliant platforms, especially since HIPAA-compliant platforms are available, and some are even free. To use a platform that is not HIPAA compliant could be seen as negligent if there is a breach investigation. If Kay did not have a HIPAA-compliant platform set up yet, she might make a decision that crossing this boundary is in the best interest of her client and even resolves continuity of care. After all, it takes time to set everything up for the complaint use of technology. Or she might decide to refer her client to a qualified TMH provider until she is ready to provide legal and ethical services to her clients.

You'll recall that Andrew asked Kay if she would look at his wife's Facebook account without her permission. There are different ways to look at this. One is through the lens of the code of ethics, which states that this is not allowed without permission from the client, so it is unethical. Andrew, however, does not think it is unethical. His argument is that his wife's Facebook account is public, so it is free for anyone to read. He also sees this as a way to seek help for his relationship by gaining understanding of the comments his wife posted.

Questions to consider:

What would you do if the mother of your 13-year-old client asked you to read his Facebook to see the comments made about his relationships, which show he is being bullied?

Your client sends you a text message late at night. What would you do?

_____

_____

A client blogs about her struggle with her sexuality and wants you to read her blog. To do this, you must create an account. What would you do?

_____

_____

You are in a recovery program and belong to an online support group where you regularly post your struggles. A client accessed the group and read your postings. How would you handle this?

_____

_____

Most of these boundary challenges are addressed in the code of ethics, as well as the standards set in your profession. For instance, when social workers use technology to communicate with clients, it can only be for professional purposes and only after the client has signed a consent. In addition, social workers must refrain from accepting "friend" requests on social media or responding to blogs. The only time this is okay is when it is part of the treatment plan. This is a standard for most mental health professionals as well because it keeps the boundaries clear.

Another boundary to keep straight is to be cautious about what you post on social media, even on your personal accounts. Your clients may search for your accounts, read this information, and become concerned or even confused by what you post. I know of a situation where an extremely gifted substance abuse counselor posted pictures of himself drinking beer with his buddies at the local bar on a social media account, and it caused negative feelings in his substance abuse group. One of the participants saw the posts and brought them to the next group meeting for everyone to see. We are always called to set good examples. The world is watching due to technology.

As I am writing this section, there is looting, rioting, and protesting going on all over the country. In the midst of all this, someone I know posted her opinion about local events on her Facebook page. This posting caused such a stir that she immediately lost two clients. Clinicians must be careful what they post on social media. I choose not to post about topics that have to do with race, ethnicity, gender identity, politics, or other issues that might inspire dismay. These comments can cause harm to the lives of those who read them, and it may reach my clients. According to the code of ethics, causing harm is against our principles.

> *"The time is always right to do what is right."*
> —Martin Luther King, Jr.

Another boundary crossing can occur with dual relationships. Using technology in certain ways can create the impression that a relationship differs from its original intention. For instance, when you receive a text message from a client, and they use emoticons, it gives the impression that this communication is from a friend or a family member. Emoticons are not used in professional documentation, and all communication from our clients is professional in nature. In addition, the code of ethics states that we must document all communications from our clients, and we certainly do not include emoticons. At the same time, I am aware that everything is not black and white. Some clients use emoticons to show their feelings when using technology and, in that case, it is different.

When therapists conduct video sessions from their home, it can make the session (and the therapeutic relationship) feel more relaxed and not as professional. Having an informed consent discussion at the onset of using technology helps with that by clarifying boundaries. Set the boundaries about the relationship right from the start, and include your social media policy, as well as your policy on acceptable forms of communication.

Questions to consider:

What boundaries do you need to set using technology?

How can you accomplish this?

_____

_____

What phone will you use for work, and how will you protect it?

_____

_____

When setting up a practice in your home, make sure you do not relax your boundaries just because your office is only accessible by family. You still want to keep PHI private, lock up your devices, and set up physical safeguards to protect your equipment, records, and communications from your clients. You also want to maintain good security with your internet system so breaches are minimal, if any.

While researching information to include in this section, I came across a book on boundaries that I wanted to share. It was not specifically written for TMH, but the information included is applicable to our practices. The book was written to include information from over forty guest authors, and it covers many topics on boundary issues for mental health professionals. If you are interested in reading more on this topic, look in the resources section for the title *Boundary Issues in Counseling*. Although the accompanying website I have provided does not include the book, it does show the contents of the book.

3

Setting Up Your Practice

In this section, I will cover the importance of choosing an internet provider, completing an assessment of needs, selecting a telehealth platform, and engaging in best practices for professionalism, including how to set up for success using videoconferencing. I will also provide some helpful checklists to assist you in setting up your practice.

Choosing a Platform

Many years ago, when I first started realizing that TMH was an option that solved problems for my clients, the only platform available was Skype. At that time, Skype offered free video conferencing, messaging, and the option of sharing files and screens. I only needed video conferencing because I maintained my own records and used my own billing system. Skype was also the platform available when I needed to complete investigations for the court at a distance. This solved the problem of time, travel, and the not-so-enjoyable body checks that occurred to enter the prison.

Later, as a clinical therapist, I had a client who moved to another part of the state, so I began using Skype to solve the distance problem. Skype was the only platform that I knew was available at that time. Conducting therapy sessions using video was unheard of in my area, and many questioned how that worked out. That is when my research began on the many legal and ethical elements of providing services from a distance.

Presently, there are many choices to consider for platforms, so there is no reason to use one that is not HIPAA compliant. Well, that was until we had the national public health emergency due to the COVID-19 pandemic. During the emergency declaration, it was permissible to use specific mediums that were not HIPAA compliant, such as Facetime and Skype.

Both of these platforms are extremely easy to use and have services that are consistent with what a clinician needs to have a quality video session. However, when there is not a state of emergency, these choices are not permitted. That is because these platforms permit their owner companies (Microsoft for Skype and Apple for Facetime) to unlock the encryption and see and hear the calls they transmit. This fact, along with the fact that they do not sign a BAA, means that clinicians are in violation of HIPAA should they decide to use either platform for TMH in any situation other than an emergency that has been approved both legally and ethically.

Many of the available platforms today were designed by mental health specialists, so they take into consideration the needs of our profession. The question that frequently comes up when I present seminars on using technology is "How do you know which platform to use?"

The best way to know is to complete an assessment of needs. In the next section, I include an explanation of what that is, and I will provide you with an example of an assessment to use for determining your platform needs. On the next page, I have also provided you with a simple form to begin the process of setting up your TMH practice. Blank spaces are provided to add additional tasks as needed.

Setting Up a Telemental Health Practice

Task	Date Started	Date Completed
Obtain license		
Purchase computer		
Install camera		
Choose internet provider		
Select platform		
Prepare office space		
Assign risk manager(s)		
Complete risk assessment		
Write policies and procedures		
Determine safety plans		
Compile risk management manual		
Create telemental health forms		
Obtain telemental health certification		
Purchase liability insurance		

Notes:

_____

_____

_____

Assessment of Needs

Before searching for the platform that meets the requirements of your practice, completing an assessment of needs can be extremely useful and will save you time. Each clinician will most likely have different needs in this area. Some professionals will require safe video conferencing, and others will only require record keeping. Many clinicians find it helpful to have insurance billing included, and others want to collect payments using credit cards. Platforms differ in the services they offer, and there are many options available. Deciding what services are necessary to sustain a mental health practice can be time-consuming, so any way to make it easier can lessen the load. Plus, it is difficult to know all the services available when you first start this journey, which is why I have designed and included an assessment of platform needs you can use for this purpose.

Once a clinician has decided what services they require, the process is much simpler. When I decided to search for a platform, I knew it was going to take some research and reading, so I went to my favorite coffee shop, ordered a delicious coffee drink, found a comfortable place to set up my computer, and started my search. This made it a more pleasant time, and I was able to enjoy the process.

First, I looked for the platforms that offered a free trial. Some offer a free trial but do not offer a free service. Some offer a free service but not a free trial. I started with the free trial and tried out a few platforms with friends and family as practice to determine which one I liked the best based on my needs. The platforms did not require any payment information while I was using the free trial to evaluate their services, so this was helpful and appreciated.

During this process, I found that I preferred a real person assisting with my questions, so that was important to know since some platforms do not have that service. Some only offer messaging and emails to answer questions. However, most platforms have some type of training that ranges from personal assistance through phone calls that include screen sharing to webinars you can watch and material you can read. When you use the free trial, you can find all this out. In addition, you can get a lot of this information by looking at the homepage on each platform's website.

To help you get started with your search, I have provided a list of platforms that claim to be HIPAA compliant. I have also included a checklist to offer guidance and assist you in choosing the one that offers the services that will work for you. I have included extra spaces on this checklist so you can add any additional services you require. There are other platforms not listed on these checklists or in this section, so feel free to continue your search. I am not proposing that any are better than the others.

My sole intention is to guide you and save you valuable time. If you are just beginning, this will help because it gives you information on what services are offered and who offers the services. Feel free to use the checklists in whatever way works best for you in your practice. Services are ever-changing with platforms, so doing a search is needed given that things can change rapidly with technology. Having a strong desire to use technology can keep you interested in moving forward with a positive frame of mind.

> *"The greatest discovery of all time is that a person can change his future by merely changing his attitude."*
>
> —Oprah Winfrey

Platform Needs Assessment

Needs	Yes	No	Maybe
Inpatient			
Residential			
Multi-provider practice			
Single-provider practice			
Video sessions			
Free service			
Free trial			
Monthly subscription			
Annual subscription			
One-time fee			
Accounting and billing			
Appointment reminders			
Appointment scheduling			
Claims management			
Client portal			
Compliance tracking			
Credit card use			
E-Prescribing			
EMR/EHR			
Employee management			
Group capabilities			
HIPAA BAA			
Initial assessments			
Intake forms			
Recording			
Screen sharing			
Training			
Treatment plans			
Website services			

Telemental Health Platforms

	Doxy.me	Thera Nest	Simple Practice	Thera LINK	Thera Platform	Thera Soft	V See	Coun Sol	We Counsel
HIPAA BAA									
Inpatient									
Residential									
Multi-provider practice									
Single-provider practice									
Video sessions									
Free service									
Free trial									
Monthly subscription									
Annual subscription									
One-time fee									
Accounting and billing									
Appointment handling									
Claims management									
Client portal									
Compliance tracking									
Credit card use									
E-Prescribing									
EMR/EHR									
Employee management									
Group capabilities									
Initial assessments									
Intake forms									
Recording									
Screen sharing									
Training									
Treatment plans									
Website services									

Notes:

_____

_____

_____

Best Practices for Professionalism

Physical Location/Room Requirements

When clinicians choose a room to provide video conferencing, it is important to ensure that the room can remain private for the duration of the session. If you hold a session at a business location, take every precaution to ensure that there is no unauthorized access to the room during the active session and otherwise. If the room is in a location where others in the building can hear the conversation, place a sound machine outside of the door to mask the communication should others be in close proximity. In addition, the use of headphones or earbuds can keep the client's voice completely private to anyone who might be close to the therapy room. I use headphones for every session, even when I am alone, because I can hear the client better and it encourages my client to use them as well. You also never know when someone might walk by or come into the room. It is an extra precaution that also safeguards my clients' privacy.

In addition, family presence can be a risk factor when you hold sessions in your home. Therefore, in addition to taking the previous precautions, you may need to alter the time of the sessions so no one is at home. Again, I use headphones and choose to use a sound machine outside of the door where I hold sessions to eliminate the confidentiality risk. I also place a sign on the door letting my family know that a session is in progress.

When you have children at home who are not the type to stay silent for any length of time, you may need to make accommodations for when you have scheduled sessions. Doing sessions at home also means you need to create your schedule based on your neighbor's lawn mowing schedule. In our neighborhood, nearby lawns are mowed before 10 in the morning, so I try to schedule my appointments after that time. In addition, be aware of noise from fans, air conditioners, and other sources of noise from nearby rooms. Bottom line: Know your surroundings when scheduling your sessions, and do your best to eliminate the extra noise.

Lighting

When setting up your office at work or at home, there are other elements you need to consider, such as color and lighting. You may want to avoid patterns or wallpaper in the background because this can be distracting and can even use up more data during videoconferencing or when recording. Solid blue or gray walls are best because blue enhances skin tone. Take precautions to keep other screens or reflective items out of the frame because they can be distracting too.

Fluorescent lighting is better for videos when you use bulbs that range from 3200 to 4700 degrees Kelvin; however, the placement is important. If the lights are on the ceiling immediately above you and directed down, this can darken yours eyes. It is best to use indirect lighting. One way to do this is to direct the lights to bounce off the ceiling. You can also place a light directly in front of you (or behind the computer facing you) and adjust. I place a lamp with a shade on it behind my computer, which works well. When the lighting is directly behind you, it will cause you to appear dark.

Some people choose to purchase a light ring and place it in front of them or behind their computer. Many people who make YouTube videos or recordings of songs use these rings. You may have noticed this if you watched *The Voice* during the pandemic, where the participants had to sing from their homes. Most of them were sent one of these rings. I have used one before for recordings, but they are not too comfortable to stare into. I prefer a lamp with a shade. You also want to make sure to block some sun from coming in through the windows so it does not shadow you in the video sessions.

Camera Placement

When choosing a camera, many new computers are equipped with webcams that do a great job. Since you will be using the camera for work, you need to use updated equipment to ensure greater clarity of projection and sound. Actually, the code of ethics requires that clinicians use updated equipment. Here is a good reason to get that new computer you might have been thinking of that has a good quality camera. Having a camera that can zoom in and out is helpful to observe your client's affect, body language, or to simply include more in the picture. This requires purchasing a camera that can attach to your computer or device. When you purchase one, look for a camera with high definition. Consult with your local experts, and document what they suggest.

When setting up and adjusting the camera for a session, frame the client in the picture slightly left of the center. That will allow space for the picture-in-picture of you to show up in the frame without covering up the client. If more than one client is attending the session, ask the clients to place their chairs close together to get them both in the frame. Another method is to have the clients sit farther away from the camera. This is best when providing group video sessions, especially when the clinician needs to observe body language. Fill the camera with people rather than objects. It may be also a good option to use a white balance screen depending on the camera, location, and lighting. You can purchase this item at camera stores, and it is not costly.

Dress Attire

Dressing for success may seem like an unnecessary topic to discuss, but it really is because I have heard some tall tales about this topic. One participant in a seminar shared that during a video session with a client, she was wearing a jacket and blouse and pajama bottoms, and her fire alarm went off. She jumped up to turn it off, and the client could see that she was in her pajamas from the waist down. This was a new client, and you can only imagine what his first impression was. Maybe it was not a good one. And maybe it hindered the professional image and even the relationship. I will let you guess on that one.

During the informed consent discussion, I always talk about dress attire, and I tell clients that even though we are enjoying the benefit of having the session from our homes, it is still a professional appointment. I inform them that I will be dressed professionally, and I ask that they dress as if they were coming to see me in my office. I have not had anyone join a session in their pajamas, but I have had some with their hair in towels. I am okay with this if they are dressed. Flexibility is necessary but not for appropriate dress. You do not want someone showing up shirtless or in their negligee.

When dressing for sessions, solids are a better choice. Checkers, plaids, and bright colors may cause blurred videos because the colors may bleed. Remember that blue enhances natural skin tones. That could be why those gowns in the examining rooms at hospitals and doctor's offices are blue. It gives the doctors a more realistic view of the skin tone. (Please do not quote me on that.) The techniques and information I have shared in this section are samples of what has worked for others, but it is up to each clinician to determine what works best for them. These are guidelines to help you start the process to determine what policies and procedures to use for your personal clinical practice or for your organization.

"The path to success is to take massive, determined action."

—Tony Robbins

4

Treatment Adaptations and Techniques

In this section, I will discuss treatment modifications and techniques to improve professionalism when using TMH. Having a good practice is not only about setting everything up in the best way possible by choosing a HIPAA-compliant platform, putting policies and procedures in place, and completing training. Clinicians must also understand how the chosen technology may challenge some skills that normally work for an in-person session but may need modification for TMH sessions. There are some best practices and adaptations that have shown success with different populations, so a review of those techniques is part of this section. This section will also look at techniques to establish a solid rapport and therapeutic alliance during TMH sessions.

Building Rapport

Research states that when clients have a good relationship with their therapists, they stay engaged longer and take a more active role in the therapeutic process. It has been known for decades that a strong therapeutic alliance can improve therapy outcomes. The particular treatment modality that a clinician uses, as well as their years of experience, are not as important as the strength of the therapeutic relationship. Therefore, building strong rapport with clients is paramount.

Case Study
IS THE CLIENT SAFE?

Janice, a psychologist in a small town, is using video sessions to see Cindy, age 25, who came in for treatment for sleep issues and panic attacks. During the initial assessment, Cindy shares that she has never experienced panic attacks before and is concerned. Her physician told her that she needed to see a counselor because there was nothing physically wrong with her, and she does not want to take medications.

During the second session, Cindy feels a little more comfortable with Janice and admits that her boyfriend of six months has recently started monitoring her phone calls. He claims that he wants to be sure she is not being hacked. At first, Cindy thought this was unusual, but she decided to believe that it was okay because he was trying to protect her. However, last week, he found a message from a male friend and reacted negatively. After she quickly explained that the message was from her cousin, he apologized. Cindy does not share the details of how her boyfriend reacted negatively. Cindy is now finding it difficult to sleep at night and is not sure if it has anything to do with her present relationship. She only knows that she wants the panic attacks to stop.

Building therapeutic rapport with Cindy is important to produce a trusting relationship that motivates Cindy to participate in the change process. Cindy could benefit from adopting healthy boundaries in relationships, but for her to hear this feedback, she needs the therapeutic relationship to be one of empathy and concern. To build rapport with Cindy, Janice was clear on her accessibility from the beginning of the relationship. She let Cindy know how to contact her and when calls would be returned. Since Cindy was seeking treatment via video sessions, Janice wanted to know if Cindy had any concerns so she could address them. This helped Cindy feel cared about and supported.

It is easier to see a client's emotions during a video session because you can observe the client's facial expressions and body responses. Sometimes, a video session brings the clinician and the client in closer proximity than they would be in person, which allows you to better monitor their empathetic expressions. However, if there are circumstances when you need to use the telephone to conduct sessions with clients, it is important to use active listening because clients cannot see your facial expressions or your body language to determine how engaged you are. For example, Cindy could not use video for one session because she had to leave her home to call in, so Janice used more paraphrasing and summaries. That way, Cindy would know Janice was listening to her, and it also ensured that Janice understood what Cindy was saying.

During one session, Janice asked Cindy how she was doing, and she became very fidgety. She avoided eye contact and began to look away from the screen. Janice wanted to increase Cindy's comfort with technology, so she did not insist on eye contact. Placing the camera in a position for your client's comfort can assist in building rapport because it shows you care about their comfort level. Eye contact is still considered essential in most cultures, but there are some groups that consider it not as important and even disrespectful. In addition, adjusting the camera as necessary may help build a trusting relationship between you and your client.

When using technology, make sure to use good equipment, such as a good camera, clear microphones and speaker system, and an internet service that does not have lag or cut off. Make sure the microphones have sufficient sensitivity and placement to clearly detect the client's speech. It would be difficult to build a strong relationship if all these things were out of order.

In addition, set up a backup system for technology failures, such as internet disconnect. Janice had discussed a backup plan with Cindy prior to beginning video sessions and had also informed her that it was acceptable to use the phone when she could not access video sessions. This information helped Cindy have more trust and less anxiety about using technology for treatment. Covering all these topics during the initial visit and discussing them during the informed consent process helps clients feel more comfortable. Clients usually appreciate understanding what is expected and knowing how things are handled. This helps to build strong rapport, especially when the clinician always remains consistent with how things are handled. An important person in my life told me to always let my word be my word. This rings true when you are working toward building a relationship and a safe environment for those who need treatment.

Cultural Considerations

Technology-based treatments have most of the same considerations as in-person treatments. In addition to the typical treatment considerations, consider what populations you want to deliver services to. Once you decide what populations you or your organization will serve, it is important to conduct a strength and needs assessment of these populations. A great way to assess the needs of a specific population is to include that population in a committee, especially if they have formerly received treatment using technology, because they can provide great input. This can drive your decisions on what programs to implement and what technology to use. It will also assist in setting up protocol, policies, and procedures to implement the most effective modalities for these chosen populations.

It is much easier to implement new technology and new programs when you have support and assistance available. For instance, if you or your agency decide to serve a population that speaks another language, you must have translators available. If you decide to serve hearing-impaired clients, then you need the proper equipment to assist that population. In addition, you must be trained on how to use the different equipment and understand how to use it.

When serving different cultures, most interventions for in-person treatment also apply to technology-based interventions. The focus is to determine whether the technology is suitable for each client according to their needs. For example, you may not want to use text-based communication with someone who does not read or write in the same language as you. You may also want to consider using larger print for those who have difficulty reading small print.

Another cultural consideration is whether you take pictures of clients for your files. This issue reminds me of a Native American gentleman I spoke with a few years ago. He was not a client, yet the conversation seems significant to this topic. I spent about two hours talking to him, and when we were saying goodbye, I asked if I could take his picture. He became very serious and asked me where the picture was going. I had never thought of that before, so I had to think for a while. I told him I would possibly use it in my classes to teach students. He responded by telling me that I could take the picture when he was not looking. I chose not to take the picture and thanked him for his time. I later read that some Native Americans believe their soul is in pictures. I love and respect this because I am a photography enthusiast, and I use photography for therapy. I now always ask about and explain any pictures I may need to take for my client's files. Respect goes a long way in building rapport and gaining trust.

Questions to consider:

What populations will you serve?

_____

_____

What technologies will work best for this population?

_____

_____

What support is necessary to implement these technologies?

_____

_____

What training do you need to provide these services with competence?

_____

_____

Older Adults

Some clinicians may believe that certain age groups are not interested in using technology, but this reminds me of a story concerning my mother-in-law. One day, she came home from work and announced that it was time for her to retire because the company she worked for was moving all her work to a computer system. She stated that she did not believe she could learn to use computers and was therefore ready to give her notice.

My mother-in-law was a strong woman, though, so after her initial resistance, she decided to try to learn how to use the computer system at work. She ended up learning the new skills needed and, with the help of some highly patient employees at the organization, learned how to do her job using technology. Later, the family bought her a laptop and even later a tablet to use for reading books. Technology became the new normal, and she grew comfortable with using it. She even obtained (and regularly used) a Facebook account. This story shows the importance of staying clear of judgments regarding what a person can and cannot do based on their age. We can choose to empower our clients by using patience and finding other ways to make adaptations to provide services using technology.

When working with older adults, you may need to use larger visuals due to changing eyesight with visual limitations. Not addressing these concerns may discourage clients from using technology for treatment, so resolving the issues is the answer. For those with hearing impairments, the resolution may be as simple as turning the volume up or adjusting the volume so they can hear what is said with clarity. Another way to turn the volume up is to use headphones, many of which are designed for individuals with hearing loss. Having this information and knowing where to find the products will help you serve older adults and make it easier for them to participate.

Check with insurance companies because they sometimes cover the cost of equipment needed to accommodate hearing, eyesight, and other disabilities. The National Deaf-Blind Equipment Distribution Program also provides equipment for communications and internet accessibility for low-income individuals who have significant vision and hearing loss. You can research and obtain this information by visiting their website at www.iCanConnect. org. There you will find videos on how this program works and information on how to obtain communication tools for qualified clients.

Another helpful tip when working with older adults with vision or hearing loss—or even with cognitive impairment—is to use technology that is easy to use and that requires a minimal number of steps. Some platforms are not as simple as others to use. I found that it was helpful to sign up for the free trials of each platform because it allowed me to quickly realize the simplicities and complexities of each one. I was then able to determine if that particular platform would work for my practice. I found that some platforms require you to download an application and sign up for an account, while others only require that you click on the link provided. The fewer steps to take, the better.

When a client has the services of a caregiver, it is sometimes a good plan to include them in the process. Those individuals assist the client with life and are part of their care, so they may need to access the platform or participate in the sessions at some point. In fact, some seniors with memory problems, hearing difficulties, or cognitive impairment may be more apt to participate in treatment if a caretaker or family member is included in the sessions. Having another person present can also help the client remember important treatment steps and build rapport. You will need to obtain a release of information, so anticipating this need ahead of time and taking care of it can ensure the process goes smoothly for your client. Having the phone numbers of the client's care team is another step to include when developing the emergency plan, just in case there is an emergency during a session.

Since many seniors live at home by themselves, it is a good practice to engage them as much as possible and to include a lot of interaction. Seniors may be dealing with increased loneliness and may even be experiencing isolation, so allowing them to communicate freely with you is helpful for building rapport and increasing the possibility of treatment adherence. Create a video session that enables older adults to participate comfortably and safely while they are at home.

Lastly, not all seniors are lonely and not all need the extra attention, so be sure to stay open-minded. I know of many seniors who are perfectly capable of understanding and participating in TMH and other technologies. Although age is a significant factor, it does not determine how things need to be for best practices. You can obtain the information regarding your client's specific needs when you do the initial assessment of needs and have that important discussion about informed consent.

Groups

During the COVID-19 pandemic in 2020, many businesses and families learned how to use technology to host many types of virtual group gatherings. Even individuals who had never used video communication before found it a welcome way to connect with those who mattered in their lives. In fact, it became one of the only ways that families and businesses could see each other when the stay-at-home orders were enacted. Similarly, it has become apparent that therapeutic groups can happen quite successfully using technology as well.

There is already research on the use of videoconferencing for group therapy that has confirmed its benefits. Even when conducted virtually, group therapy offers the benefit of receiving treatment with others who are experiencing similar challenges, which allows clients to gain additional support and understanding. With strong leadership, group participants can build strong bonds that encourage healing.

When conducting group therapy, it is important to use evidence-based protocols to gain the best treatment outcomes. This can be done by a competent, trained clinician who uses treatment plans and protocols that match the clients' issues. Conducting an evidence-based group also requires that clinicians maintain awareness of the cultural differences among group members and make appropriate adaptations to meet any challenges. All this begins by doing a proper assessment of group participants and including only those who will gain the most benefit from the structured curriculum and from the choice of participants. Clinicians should always work within their scope of practice and only facilitate groups they have experience and training to conduct. In addition, clinicians need to be aware of each client's needs and expectations regarding group therapy via video sessions, and they must document the strategies used to determine the effectiveness of the treatment.

When setting up the video sessions, confirm that the space you will use is free of distractions so everyone can speak freely. You also want to make sure that the internet connection is secure and not public. To prevent the Wi-Fi from shutting down, connect directly into the modem using the proper connections. Places like Best Buy, as well as other stores that sell technology, can assist with the cords and connections needed for your type of computer and router.

Ask group attendees to turn their phones on airplane mode to eliminate interruptions during the session. In addition, ask them to wear headphones during the session because this keeps people in other rooms from hearing the conversations. Some group leaders make the use of headphones mandatory to ensure the privacy of the other group members. If everyone is using headphones, participants know that others nearby will not be able to hear what they share.

If headphones are not available, ask members to turn the volume down to the lowest possible level. Have a policy or guideline that explains what to do when someone gets disconnected, such as allowing them to call in using their telephone if the internet goes out at their location. You will want to discuss these guidelines and have the group come to an agreement when establishing them.

During the initial conversation, you also want to establish guidelines that explain what to do if someone walks in the room who is not authorized to be there. This is considered a breach of privacy. If there are breaches, group members may be less willing to continue with the video sessions, causing them to drop out before they complete treatment. Informed consent establishes the parameters of group participation using video sessions, so be sure to spend the necessary time discussing these important group policies and procedures so everyone is informed and fully consents.

When conducting groups using video sessions, another privacy concern is that there may be a permanent record of the group transcript if the platform is recording your session. Some mental health professionals choose not to permit the recording of sessions, but some platforms record the session as part of their records. In this situation, a release is needed from the client before starting the session. Also, be sure to read the small print when deciding on which platform to use. If you do not want sessions recorded, choose a platform that does not automatically save the sessions. All forms of therapy using technology have privacy concerns, and facilitating groups are no different in that respect. Staying in compliance with HIPAA remains a legal issue that you need to address.

Third parties can intercept any online communications by viewing unencrypted messages, gaining access to computers used during the group process, or stealing passwords. A way to assist with this is to use messaging that is encrypted and to make sure to use strong passwords that are changed regularly. In addition, review with the group participants how they can do their part to secure the sessions. Group members can pose a privacy concern when they share communication outside of the group. This can occur if they are able to record the session (as previously mentioned) or if they let others watch the therapy session without letting others in the group know of their presence.

Clinicians have an ethical duty to protect their clients. Mental health practitioners are responsible for creating a safe and supportive environment that protects clients from any harm. The following case scenario shows the importance of establishing guidelines at the beginning of the group process. It also reminds us that having policies and procedures established ahead of time is essential.

Case Study
AN UNSETTLING PRIVACY BREACH

Nicole was leading a group of domestic violence survivors using video sessions. The group was going along well, and members had even made friends with one another. Since this group was held in a small town, everyone seemed to have mutual friends or acquaintances. One day during a session, Christy—a 25-year-old who was presently living with her husband who had been charged with domestic violence—got up to get some water, and her phone fell on the floor. When that happened, everyone in the session saw that Christy's husband was in the room sitting on the bed watching the entire process and hearing their conversation.

Questions to consider:

What is a good policy for privacy in group video sessions?

_____

_____

What can the policy be when there is a breach?

_____

_____

What would you do about Christy's future participation?

_____

_____

When conducting groups using video, it is a best practice to establish privacy controls and ensure group compliance. One of the first areas to cover for privacy controls is to establish client authentication. It is important to have policies and procedures on how this will happen in a group, and you will want to determine the authentication system you will use. When using a

HIPAA-compliant platform, there are authentication systems that can identify the user, but only after the clinician has identified the client who will be invited to join the video group. During the initial assessment of group members, I always ask for a driver's license to confirm that the person before me on the screen is who they say they are. To confirm location, I usually know what state my client is in, and it is a law that driver's licenses stay current. My policy is to always ask for identification and to enter this communication into my documentation.

Having further discussion about privacy and security with group participants is also important, especially when you consider the earlier case study. It is possible that Nicole, the group facilitator in this scenario, did not discuss allowing others in the room during the sessions. Because of this oversight, Christy could say that she did not know it was important. However, if Nicole had completed the informed consent process as required by some state laws and the code of ethics, then she would most likely have a better result. It is always best to outline the group rules at the beginning of the process so everything is crystal clear.

It is also always best to screen potential groups members the same as you would for an in-person session but with some additional questions. When using video, I always ask if the potential participant will have access to a private location for the sessions. I also want to know if they have the competence and even the desire to participate in video sessions. If they do not have the competence, yet they do have the desire, I want to make sure I do what I can to educate them so they can become competent. The platform I use simply requires members to click a link from their email account to join the session. It is so easy to use that it gives me the added confidence that I can make it possible for anyone who wants to be a part of the group to learn what is necessary.

It is good to structure the groups and set clear goals for each session when possible. When clients know what to expect, it relieves some of the anxiety associated with participating in a group treatment program. I want my group participants to stay engaged, so I also use small assignments to encourage them to practice between sessions. My groups are usually closed groups for a specified number of days or weeks, but many groups are open to others joining at any time because they are ongoing.

I have a friend who hosts a mindfulness group, and participants can join whenever they choose to. She informs them of the group guidelines before they sign up and has them agree to these guidelines, which works out well. This same friend also runs a grief group that is open-ended. She decides on specific topics ahead of time and completes a specific topic during each 90-minute session. She mentioned that a problem sometimes comes up when a new person is invited to join the group because they do not have the competence to use the platform or even their own technology. Given that this could be harmful to the group process, I suggested that she share a handout with instructions on how to use the platform and the chosen technology and provide this education prior to inviting them to join. This way, the client can gain some understanding that will assist them with beginning the group process.

Group video sessions are much more popular today as the world has been forever changed in light of COVID-19, and families and businesses have had to stay at home through it all. Using technology for group meetings and sessions can eliminate isolation for many and can also improve access to care.

Veterans

At times, military personnel have difficulty finding mental health services they are comfortable with. As a former Army wife, I can attest how uncomfortable it is to present with problems to someone on the base where your husband is stationed. When the base is a small one, there is a chance that the person helping you knows the enlisted person, which can be experienced as a breach of confidentiality and cause extreme discomfort.

Several years ago, I was speaking at an Army base about law and ethics and began talking about how confidentiality changes when a client expresses suicidal ideation or behaviors. I spoke about the importance of conducting an appropriate assessment to determine danger and the potential for harm if confidentiality is broken when it is not necessary. During the presentation, I noticed that a young soldier participating in the seminar (whom I will call Sergeant) appeared to express discomfort. Later, Sergeant raised his hand and said that confidentiality is not always provided in the military. I asked him to talk more about that if he was willing.

Sergeant told the group that about a year ago, he went to the Army chaplain and revealed that he was having suicidal thoughts and believed he was depressed. He was hoping the chaplain would offer some guidance on how to deal with the depression so he could feel good again. The chaplain told him he was concerned for him, prayed with him, and made another appointment for the following week. Sergeant said he was encouraged and thought he was going to get some help and support in the process.

The next day, Sergeant was called into the office of his commanding officer. The commanding officer told him that the chaplain expressed concern that he might be in danger of hurting himself. Sergeant was surprised and upset because he thought that conversation was confidential, and he was not informed that this information would be shared with anyone. He immediately felt like he was in trouble and stated that he was fine and would not talk like that again. The commanding officer responded by telling him he was now considered a threat to the entire unit and that he could not be in charge. Sergeant was given another assignment for the remainder of his time on that base.

When Sergeant shared his story, you could hear the frustration in his voice and see the sadness in his eyes. He told us that he entered the military as a lifelong career and had already reached the rank of sergeant. He had plans to continue his education and retire as an officer in twenty years or more. Now he was experiencing hopelessness and unsure how to resolve it. This situation may have been avoided if the chaplain was trained in suicide assessment. This soldier did not have a desire to act on his thoughts. He only wanted to understand why he was having those thoughts and do something about it. The chaplain and the commanding officer had the misconception that once you have suicidal thoughts you are always a risk to yourself and others, and in a position of military protection of the public, this is not acceptable.

I share this story because the stigma of mental health is real to many, and it keeps people from getting the help they need. I have heard about this perceived stigma a lot in the military population. In Sergeant's situation, the military was missing appropriate training on suicide assessment, and they needed relevant training on the topic of obtaining help for mental health concerns. Telehealth is an answer to this perceived stigma because military personnel and their families can obtain the help they need without seeing someone on base. They can search online and find a provider who will meet their needs using telemedicine and TMH. In fact, the military remains a leader in providing telehealth services. They provide more services using technology than most agencies.

Recent research has sought to determine the safety and feasibility of providing military service members and veterans care by comparing the efficacy of in-home video sessions with in-office sessions. In particular, one study—which examined the efficacy of behavioral activation treatment for depression (BATD) among military personnel—found that home-based video sessions were just as effective as in-person sessions, and sometimes the outcome for the former was even better (Luxton et al., 2016).

In the military, there is great structure, and BATD is structured as well. It gives clients assignments to accomplish, and once clients meet these goals, the sessions become shorter in duration. It is easy for clinicians to administer BATD, and the manual is located online for free. I have provided a link for this manual in the resource section of this book. Given the benefit of this in-home TMH program, it might be beneficial to hire clinicians to work different shifts to make it possible for military personnel to be at home during treatment.

In 2010, the Office of the Assistant Secretary of Defense for Health Affairs recommended that mental health providers for the Department of Defense receive appropriate evidence-based training for acute stress disorder and PTSD. When researching information to include in this guidebook, I found different trainings that are beneficial when working with the military, depending on the status of the individual needing treatment. One such training, which is provided by the Center for Deployment Psychology, carries the title of Star Behavioral Health Provider upon completion of the program. This is an evidence-based training geared toward assisting the military and their families. In addition, clinicians need training in cognitive processing therapy to provide clinical services to trauma survivors.

Implement a formal program that is evidence-based. It is most effective to use a designated coordinator who specializes in knowing how to implement and monitor evidence-based practices. This person can track innovations and ensure systematic dissemination of best practices. It is also helpful to compile a manual with evidence-based therapeutic tools that can be distributed to each clinician. Include tools and programs that have demonstrated effectiveness.

In addition, put performance measures in place to determine treatment outcomes. This allows clinicians to become familiar with the use of outcome measures so they can make necessary changes and implement new procedures. It's also helpful to have checklists available where clinicians can write progress notes. These checklists are easy to develop. Last, but not least, set up a systematic consultation process for clinicians. As providers, it is easy to get caught up in making all the decisions and doing things ourselves, when it is much more helpful to enlist the support and advice of others to ensure nothing is missed. Work with local clinics and behavioral health centers on military bases to advocate for the delivery of evidence-based interventions. Additional military resources are located in the resource section.

Case Study

AN UNFAIR (AND UNSAFE) STIGMA

Andrew, a soldier in the Air Force, was having suicidal thoughts while stationed in Afghanistan, so he went to his commanding officer seeking help. His commanding officer told him that he needed to "tough it out" because he was not allowed to show weakness in his position. Andrew had worked hard to earn his stripes and decided not to continue his search for help. He did not receive any assistance for his suicidal ideation at that time.

Months later, shortly after he returned home, he had an argument with a friend, which brought his struggles to the surface, and Andrew consequently attempted suicide. His wife found him in time, and although he is doing well today, he almost died that day. He was placed in an inpatient facility and began treatment. Andrew was intelligent and immediately learned what he needed to improve. He intellectually understood the steps needed, to get better but struggled emotionally for some time.

The perceived stigma attached to getting help in the military was real for Andrew. Although not all military leaders promote this stigma, it is often perpetuated by those who are neither well-versed in nor have an understanding of mental health issues. Upon discharge from inpatient treatment, Andrew found a TMH provider and a psychiatrist by searching online. Both of these professionals were not enlisted in the military, yet they had the training to understand how to treat those in the military. By seeing both of these professionals by using technology, he learned new coping skills, obtained the medicines that worked for him, and is doing well today.

Today, there are many treatment choices for the military and their families, although there are still many barriers for veterans to obtain mental health care. One study identified five specific barriers that exist, including: (1) concern about what others think; (2) financial, personal, and physical obstacles (e.g., health problems, homelessness, and disabilities); (3) confidence in the VA healthcare system; (4) navigating VA benefits and healthcare services; and (5) privacy, security, and abuse of services (Cheney et al., 2018).

For example, I recall a young soldier, Pat, who returned from Afghanistan with a brain injury due to an explosive. He had difficulties making decisions, trouble completing paperwork, and struggled with finding a place to live with no stable employment. Presently, Pat is on disability and lives in a mobile home park, but personal, physical, and financial barriers used to be a part of his life. Many of his problems were based on his lack of confidence in the system to meet his needs. He also had difficulty trying to find his way through the system to obtain the services he needed. Since he was already out of the military when he sought treatment, he was not affected by barriers involving concerns over what others might think or concerns about privacy. However, these barriers were certainly present in the former scenarios I discussed regarding Sergeant and Andrew.

The use of TMH offers a way to overcome these barriers. Soldiers can seek help using the internet and find specialists in the area they are struggling. They can talk to their chosen provider in the privacy of their home instead of being seen going into a military office with a sign on the door for all to see. Military personnel can also engage with providers through the VA Video Connect app and work with providers across state lines with the Anywhere to Anywhere program, both of which I discussed earlier in this book.

As a former Army wife, I had to go onto the base to receive any type of service. If I would have needed a mental health appointment, it would have been much more comfortable for me to obtain a session using technology instead of possibly running into my husband's commanding officer or his friends while on the base. He was part of the military police, and image was important to him. In addition, I was not able to leave my children at home with strangers. Searching for a female clinician online would have been more comfortable in that situation. Technology solves those problems and others when it comes to obtaining mental health services. When clinicians want to provide services for the military, it requires specialized training and education because understanding the needs of the military and having knowledge of their challenges is necessary when deciding on effective treatment approaches.

It is common for clinicians who treat veterans to work at hospitals or clinics that are connected to the VA. This is not mandatory, yet it does seem to be the norm. Keep in mind that when clinicians work with the VA, it is possible to offer therapeutic services to the military in other states with only one state license. For this to happen, your training and education must be accredited by the Council for Accreditation of Counseling and Related Educational Programs, and you must have a valid license to practice.

Using TMH successfully with the military depends on both organizational and technological issues. Not only must you be competent in the use of advanced technology when working with this population, but you must have an understanding of their lifestyle and the hardships they have endured. You must also have a strong desire to be involved in caring for the needs of military personnel and their families. You can achieve this competence in many ways. One is to simply spend time with military personnel and their families. Another is to read about their hardships and learn about treatment methods that have been shown to help. There is a lot of research to consider. There are many books written by soldiers that give a lens into the minds and lives of an active soldier and their family.

TMH can be applied to solve the needs of military personnel in many environments, whether they are deployed or are seeking sessions from home. We cannot claim to know everything about our clients' lives, yet knowing enough about their lifestyle and the hardships they have faced can assist us in building strong rapport with them and developing a treatment plan that meets their needs.

Couples and Families

We all know that we have to follow the federal and state laws and guidelines for our professions. That is the same for all mental health professions. However, when working with couples and families, it can be different when you have family members located in different states during a session. In this situation, it is mandatory to know the licensing laws of the states where your clients are, as well as the laws where you are.

In 2017, the American Association for Marriage and Family Therapy (AAMFT) wrote a report that reviewed the best practices for conducting couples and family therapy online. Throughout the report, I found it difficult to find concrete suggestions to include in this guidebook because the report was written several years ago, and at that time, there was not a lot of research that resulted in evidence-based practices for couples and family therapy. However, they wrote about practices that are beneficial to treating couples and families online. I am providing you with these best practices for marriage and family therapists as I understand them from the AAMFT. According to their report, it is a best practice to:

- Present your license to TMH clients and let them know where they can verify this information. This adds integrity to the service you provide.

- Know the role of each person in the session, and make that clear to everyone at the onset of the session. This can include family members, caretakers, or even probation officers or other mental health professionals involved in their treatment. Always make sure everyone knows one another so there are no surprises.

- Obtain a reliable internet system with broadband adequate for using TMH, and ensure it is set up to meet privacy and security standards.

- Use 256-bit encryption with all communications when it is available. It is usually available for most types of communication, including video, email, and text messaging.

- Obtain training in the use of technology so you understand how to set up sessions most effectively and conduct them using any adaptations necessary. Training will include many of the topics included in this guidebook with additional information provided. When working with families, it is important to learn additional details, such as instructing them where to put the camera so everyone can be seen and included in the sessions.

- Always include an informed consent prior to beginning treatment, which needs to include all the important elements. (See informed consent section.)

- Verify and authenticate every person involved in the session, including their age and their location at the time of the session.

- Complete an assessment of appropriateness for online services, document the results, and then monitor to see if this changes throughout the process. At times, clients may initially desire to use TMH services, but this could change after a few sessions, and they may want to continue with in-person sessions. Clients always have autonomy to change their mind, and we are ethically obliged to let them know the alternatives.

- Evaluate the client's progress, and determine if alternative treatments might bring a better result. Issues can come up during treatment where the client may need to be referred to another clinician for other services. An example would be if you are seeing a client who, after a few sessions, admits they have an eating disorder that may be serious. You may need to refer them to a doctor and, depending on the results, refer them to an eating disorder specialist.

- Allow clients and others to access the records after appropriate authentication and while following the relevant laws.

- Maintain clear boundaries during sessions and between them. This could include things like dressing appropriately, letting clients know of approved communication times, and explaining what types of devices are permitted for communication.

- Have an emergency plan with every client prior to starting the first session that includes local resources and ensures continuity of care during the crisis. After the crisis is resolved, an additional assessment of appropriateness may be needed. Documentation of everything is necessary.

- Have a backup plan when technology breaks down or fails to work for a time. For instance, discuss whether clients can use the phone to continue the session or whether an alternate clinician will become involved to continue their care. Have a discussion about who will call whom, as well as what the time factor might be during this process, so there is no confusion about what needs to happen in this situation. Review this at the beginning of each video session.

- Inform clients of any breaches as soon as possible, and offer methods for added protection for the future.

- Review technology annually, and make any revisions to the technology, policies and procedures, and security measures as needed.

- Evaluate competency and look at whether engaging in TMH practice is bringing the outcomes desired. Additional training is always a good choice. Technology is changing rapidly, and keeping up with the changes requires a commitment to keeping informed.

When engaging in TMH with couples and families, clinicians must follow all laws and relevant standards that are developed for providing therapy using technology. The AAMFT published guidelines to minimize risks to clients and clinicians in these situations, many of which are covered in this guidebook, such as compliance with the laws and the code of ethics, the use of adequate and secure networks with encryption and software for protection, advertising and marketing that follows standards set by the Federal Trade Commission, informed consent, assessments, emergency plans, technology failures and breaches, and annual accountability and reviews to evaluate your practice and equipment.

Let's consider the following case study:

Case Study

CAN THE FAMILY COME?

Louise and Craig are having difficulties in their marriage. They are both in their fifties, have two teen children, and have been married for twenty years. Louise and Craig have attended in-person counseling with Evelyn during other difficult times in their relationship. Presently, Louise and Craig are having problems communicating with their children so they want help with this and want to include their children in the sessions. Evelyn now offers both in-person sessions and video sessions, so Louise is calling to set up an appointment. She wants to know if TMH sessions can be considered.

Questions to consider:

How would you respond to Louise when she called for advice?

_____

_____

What do you need from Louise and Craig before proceeding with counseling?

_____

_____

What happens if they do not agree regarding how to proceed?

_____

_____

Evelyn remembers that this family has difficulty communicating, so together with the clients, they decide to set up a TMH session that includes the entire family. Evelyn must send new informed consent forms to the parents and also have them complete an intake form that includes information about the teenage children. She is familiar with the dynamic of this family, so she decides that it is best to put the parents in one room of the house and the teens in another room of the house on two different devices. This way, she can use the mute function to allow one person to speak at a time. The teens have a close relationship and listen to each other, but they resist listening to their parents, so using technology in this manner could prove helpful.

Before beginning, Evelyn assists the family in setting up their seating arrangements at home so that she can see and hear all of them and they can see and hear her. During this initial appointment with all four in the same room, she explains her proposed set-up and talks about the benefits of having the adults and teens in separate rooms. Once they all agree to the plan, she reviews the informed consent form for TMH and goes over the emergency plan. She then gives them time to ask questions. Evelyn sets up the appointment for the next session. If this does not work out, in-person sessions can be arranged.

When setting up a session this way, split screens can be useful. By using this approach, everyone can see and hear one another speaking without interruptions. It may take a little more time and effort to set this up with a family, but it can work well with families and in group sessions. When you mute everyone except for the person speaking, it eliminates other noise distractions that might manifest, such as movements, fans, and lawn mowers.

In the scenario with this family, it could also be helpful to have everyone on their own device, including the mother and father. This can be determined during the assessment of the family and after the first few sessions. The good news is that we have technology to help solve these problems, and it is only going to get better.

Children

The ATA recommends that when working with children, clinicians should follow the same guidelines used with adults while considering necessary modifications based on the developmental status of each child. It always amazes me how much young people know about technology. But when you consider that the children of today have never lived without it, it all makes sense. Five-year-olds know how to use Facetime, and they easily learn about how to use apps on phones and tablets. In the classroom, teachers also use technology that is interactive and inspires creativity. For example, interactive whiteboards allow children to control a computer by touching the screen. When conducting TMH, you can achieve this same whiteboard option with a good platform.

To ensure this section includes relevant adaptations for the use of TMH with children, I enlisted the assistance of Mrs. Shelly Bastean, who supervises future teachers while they are interns. Since she is an expert in working with children, I wrote this section with her help and guidance. During the time when schools and colleges were closed due to COVID-19, she was unable to observe interns working in the classroom, so she improvised by supervising interns with the use of video technology. That was the only way she could make sure they received the practice hours they needed to graduate. In order for this virtual classroom to happen, she had to develop and teach her interns the tools needed to use video conferencing effectively with children. In the following section, you will find many ideas on how to successfully use video sessions with children.

When conducting TMH with children, there is a lot of planning and preparation that needs to happen before you begin sessions. First, the room needs to be set up on both ends: yours and theirs. The room the child is in works best when it is large enough to include others in the session, such as parents or caregivers. The room also needs to have enough space so the camera can take in the child's behaviors and movements. For this to happen, you need to have a conversation with the child's parents to discuss proper set-up of the computer and the room. This way, you can observe the child's behaviors and watch their reactions.

When speaking with the parents about the room set-up, mention what items may be used and needed during the sessions, as well as what is not necessary and would be best taken out of the room. You will also want to discuss the parent or caregiver's presence during the sessions and determine if that is necessary or if it would hinder the treatment process. Children may act more independently when their parents are not present. The goal is to set the room up to facilitate a strong engagement with the child and anyone else who may be participating in the sessions.

It is also essential to set up expectations at the beginning of the clinical relationship. For instance, when a child is sitting in an office, they cannot get up and leave the session, but at home they can. Therefore, it is necessary to agree upon what will happen when the child gets up and does not stay in front of the screen. Having these norms on the forefront of the child's minds is helpful for them. Sometimes, parents also like to sit next to their children and engage with them, answer for them, and even distract them. Setting up expectations with the parents may also be necessary.

The process of setting expectations and determining guidelines is a great time to build rapport with the child and with the parents. It is one of your first conversations, so it is a good time to establish boundaries and the benefits of the treatment.

Questions to consider:

Do you want the parents in the sessions?

_____

_____

When will they participate?

_____

_____

How will they participate?

_____

_____

When discussing expectations and boundaries, there are ways to make this process more interactive for children. For example, you can use a poster board to make the guidelines and boundaries more visible. As information is shared and agreed upon by all parties, the agreements can be placed on a poster board at both your location and the client's location. Of course, the child must be equipped with the ability to negotiate and have discussions of this nature. If they are not, initiate this with the parents or the caretakers. You may need to revisit these guidelines during the sessions to reestablish the boundaries.

There are other ways to make this an enjoyable process for children. Depending on the child's age, you can use a chart that states how you will talk to each other and pull it up when needed in a session. You can even use puppets, stuffed animals, and short stories. Make sure you are prepared if the child has limitations, such as those with regard to hearing, eyesight, and reading abilities.

Do not be afraid to let children know what you need them to do. When they are distracted and away from the screen, tell them to move closer, and help them know where it is best for them to be. You can use humor and show them how it looks when you are off to the side (possibly using hide-and-seek to illustrate this to younger children).

To encourage the behavior needed to pursue treatment, you can also find out the things the child values and use these for rewards and motivation as needed. When setting up a rewards system, you can have the rewards come from you or from the parents. For example, if the reward is coming from the parent, you might say, "Mommy said you could go to the park if you completed the assignment with me today." If the reward is coming from you, it might sound like, "Let's add a happy sticker to your poster today for how well you did during our time together." Always plan ahead with a purposeful plan that fits into the treatment goals so that you are prepared to respond to the different situations that may occur. This will add to your confidence and your competence in working with your clients and their families and caretakers.

Questions to consider:

What will you do if the child reacts by crying?

_____

_____

What will you do if the child is not attentive?

_____

_____

What will you do if the child misbehaves?

_____

_____

After you set up the room and establish guidelines with both the child and others involved, consider the treatment plan that will meet the objectives of the session. Knowing the strategies that will accomplish your session goals will assist you in knowing what supplies you need. You may need to purchase supplies and send them to the child, or the parent may have to purchase them and have them ready in time for the session. You may also need to mail or email certain supplies to the parent so they can print them before the sessions. This can only happen when the parents are cooperative and willing to follow through with the necessary planning and arrangements. When parents are cooperative, you can suggest certain things be present during the sessions, such as a stuffed animal or a specific book or game. It is much better to find ways to engage children with concrete things to accomplish the treatment goals.

When you are working with younger children, such as 5-year-olds, it is helpful to be animated and to engage the children physically. For example, you can use the supplies that you sent to the parent ahead of time and have the children point to them or show them. They could also point on the screen or read out loud. They can trace with markers, cut things out, or glue things when the parents cooperate and set things up ahead of time. If not, it can prove helpful to use a platform that has a shared screen and that allows you to teach the child through an interactive whiteboard. When these things are not available, engaging them with simple questions can work, such as "Can you see the sun?" or "How does the sun feel today?" or "Show me your favorite color."

If your technology allows for screen sharing, another activity is to watch videos with the child. It is also a good idea to watch short character videos with young children. Depending on their age, they may only be able to sit and focus for a few minutes. For older children, you can watch longer videos because some older children can stay focused longer. You can always stop the videos to engage with the child and even participate in physical activities together, such as the happy dance when something good happens or when the session is over.

Case Study
TELEMENTAL HEALTH WITH KIDS

Warner set up video sessions with Marie because his 7-year-old son, Patrick, was being bullied at school and was acting out on his little sister at home. Warner wanted Marie to help Patrick with assertiveness skills and anger management. Marie read a story about *Angry Arthur* to Patrick during the second session because he did not want to talk. She showed him pictures and engaged him through the screen with questions about the story. During one of the video sessions, Patrick became angry and threw his pencil across the room at his sister when she entered the room.

Using a common storybook with characters, especially for younger clients, is helpful because they can connect with the characters, and that can be used to further the goal of the session. For example, the book *Angry Arthur* makes a good point about how we sometimes get so angry that we do things and forget what we are angry about. Today, Marie's goal is to practice the coping skills Patrick learned last week when she read him the book. She wants him to leave the session knowing how to breathe and calm himself down, as well as to think about why he gets so upset before he overreacts. When Patrick became angry during the session, Marie stated, "Remember the story about *Angry Arthur*? What do you think he would do right now? Do you think he would stop and take some deep breaths to help him not get so upset?"

In addition, have a plan with a definite objective that you would like the child to meet in each session. Always have a plan of what you want the child to walk away with when they leave the session. Teach them the strategy, model it, and have them do it independently so that by the end of the session, you can access what they have accomplished, validate their good behavior, and even reward them with a sticker on the poster.

For example, if Patrick starts to get fidgety and there are still ten more minutes left, Marie can bring the guidelines poster into view and say, "Here is our poster where we wrote down all the things that were going to help us in our time together. We only have ten minutes left, so I need you to stay in your seat for ten more minutes." Another way Marie could handle this situation is to have some stretches ready. A one-minute stretch break, or even that famous happy dance, can bring back enough energy to finish the session.

It is important to know what works for children so you can gain their attention back when it strays. With some children, you can merely discuss the lack of attention and ask them what they can do to help them remember to focus. Younger children might say they just want to color. Doing so can keep them engaged, and the sheets they color can relate to the treatment goals. Other children may need visuals, such as a poster or physical symbol, like putting a finger to their nose. Still others might benefit from using a cue word that reminds them that they need to focus their attention for a little while longer. Marie and Patrick use the cue word *dragons* because Patrick likes to draw them and has books about them. It reminds him how he can focus when he wants to. The choices will depend on the developmental age of the child. Older children can usually have a discussion, and younger children may need to get up and dance for a minute.

It is also important to consider how much time you need for each planned activity. Should the activity take more time than allotted, have a plan on what to do to end the activity before it is completed. If a child finishes too quickly, plan to have other options that relate to the treatment goals. Positive reinforcement inspires more good behavior, so always think ahead about what activities or words will tell the children they are doing things successfully.

When working with children about their feelings through the use of videoconferencing, they may not always have the words to express what they want to say, just as they might not in person. Giving children the words to describe their feelings at a time when they are experiencing them is more authentic and beneficial for younger children. For instance, when Patrick is talking about his sister in an angry tone with a scowl on his face, Marie can say, "Are you feeling angry right now?"

Marie could also refer to the pictures in the book that show Arthur when he is angry and relate those expressions to how Patrick is showing emotion. She needs to give Patrick time to think before interrupting him, or he will have to start the thinking process all over again. Marie waited a long time for Patrick to respond, so she eventually said, "Patrick, do you need more time, or do you need me to ask the question in a different way?"

Most clinicians use their language as a model for children. This remains the same with video sessions. In addition, visuals have consistently been used with children. Adding them to video sessions keeps them engaged. Clinicians may have to be more creative on how that happens, but it is worth the extra effort. Adding visuals, like pictures in a book or on the screen, helps keep them stay involved so that they leave with increased coping skills. It is good to prepare for this.

"Before anything else, preparation is the key to success."
—Alexander Graham Bell

5

Business Considerations

Marketing and Advertising

In this section, I provide guidance on the process of advertising and marketing a TMH practice, including legal issues and ethical concerns. I will address some of the laws concerning advertising and discuss how to identify problems and challenges of promoting a TMH practice. After that, I look at the options to address these challenges in business and how to advertise and market services to maximize results. By the end of this section, you will understand what you need to advertise your practice successfully.

Questions to consider:

What populations do you want to serve?

_____

_____

What services will you offer?

_____

_____

How do you want to obtain clients?

_____

_____

What is the budget for marketing?

_____

_____

Since you are choosing to use technology, you may want to consider an online presence by creating a website. This provides a place for clients to find a description of the services you offer, your professional credentials, the populations you serve, and any specialties, such as anger management or dialectical behavioral therapy. When designing a website, make sure that it appears professional and does not have a casual appearance. Clients looking for a clinician may not want to see a picture of their potential therapist on the beach drinking a margarita.

I attempted to design my own website a couple of times. The first time, I paid an annual fee and did all the designing myself, but since this was my first time, I did not understand how to make the website accessible so it could be seen by as many people as possible. The second time, I used a well-known website that took care of the marketing, and I had much better results. There are professionals who will help you with all of this, and it is worth the investment, depending on what you want to accomplish. Although I learned from this experience, it might have been a better choice to consult with an expert from the start instead of trying to save money by doing it myself. An expert can create a website based on your criteria, and they can set up the technology in a way that puts your website at the top of internet searches. An expert also knows how to set up your website so internet searches attract the type of clients you want to gain attention from.

Finally, when setting up a website, have links to the professional code of ethics of your profession, your state licensing board, and any other professional organizations you belong to. This helps potential clients gain confidence in you, and it increases your validity as a professional. For social workers, the code of ethics actually requires that they include these professional links.

Having a social media presence is another helpful marketing tool. Some clinicians have built a Facebook page to share self-help techniques and strategies for coping. However, some professional codes of ethics, such as the American Counseling Association, warn that clinicians are to avoid social media with clients. Since I am a licensed counselor, I have interpreted that to mean that I cannot interact with clients on social media. If I were to use social media for marketing, I would not respond to clients using social media. I would inform my potential clients that if they wanted to contact me for services, they could either email me at my business address through a secure platform or call me at my business phone number.

When advertising your services and your credentials, always make sure that all statements on your web pages are an honest representation of who you are and what you offer. I have had clinicians tell me that they see clients in other states but advertise these services as "coaching." Although we are permitted to offer services that do not require licensure, we must be sure that we are not crossing that boundary from coaching to counseling. This would be a legal issue and an ethical issue.

When I first moved to Florida, I was licensed in Illinois and was unable to practice in Florida because of different educational requirements for licensing in this state. Now my daughter has a master's degree in education and is a certified educational coach. She could have opened an office in Florida easily and advertised it as "educational coaching." I now have my Florida license, but to offer coaching, I would need to make it clear what that means, or I would be advertising deceptively, which is against federal law.

According to the Federal Trade Commission, there can be no deceptive statements when advertising online. For instance, clinicians must state their credentials appropriately and only advertise the services they can provide with said licenses and certifications. This applies to interns as well. If you have interns working in your TMH practice or otherwise, you must note this on your website or advertising platform so clients are aware of who will be providing the service. When interns are providing services to clients under supervision at your organization, include the name of their supervisor and the license of their supervisor on your website.

After setting up your website, a way to gain the contact information of potential clients is to offer a free eBook or free handouts when they enter their email or phone number. I am sure you have given your email address to access certain information on the web—or maybe not, but this is a way for organizations to contact you after you visit their site.

There are many free resources you can use to inspire clients to consider contacting you for services, such as using Twitter. At the last American

Counseling Association conference, they had a break-out group that discussed how to use social media to advertise a practice. It was quite interesting and included many options and lots of great advice, such as the time of day to post on Twitter to get the most response and how to connect large groups of people to existing accounts. This information is beyond the scope of this book, but I wanted you to know that it is possible should you desire to go all out with advertising. When you choose to advertise using these methods, be prepared because you never know when something might go viral.

Business cards are a simple and easy way to advertise and market your practice, so having them with you always is a good idea. You never know when you might meet a potential client or a person who is searching for a clinician for someone else. When designing your cards, there are many online services that make it easy. They allow you to choose the art, fonts, and words—and the cost is minimal. When you make your own cards, you want to make sure all the information on the cards is correct and that it clearly states your credentials along with your services.

It is also unethical to solicit client statements for advertising or marketing. Even if a client is no longer using your services, this can be misunderstood as a dual relationship or even exploitation. Therefore, it is a best practice not to solicit marketing statements from past or present clients. Some clinicians have chosen to use statements from clients without identifying them, but in a small town that could propose a problem.

It is important to know what the state laws are concerning marketing your practice. Since each state differs in their laws, it is necessary to know the laws in the state in which you are advertising.

Questions to consider:

Is there a parity law to cover TMH in your state?

_____

_____

If you are reaching out to other states, do you need a license in that state to practice?

_____

_____

What does your licensing state have to say about that?

_____

_____

Insurance

Many states require insurance companies to cover services provided using TMH. Some states also require insurance companies to reimburse clinicians at the same rate as an in-person session. Clinicians may need to provide additional documentation to receive payment for the provision of TMH services, so knowing what to document becomes important. Since the COVID-19 pandemic, things have changed in this regard. Instead of many states requiring insurance companies to cover TMH services, it has changed such that *most* states now require coverage.

The benefit of using technology exploded during this pandemic, and businesses began to change the way they provided services to meet client demands in a more efficient and sometimes better way. Of course, when taking a client's insurance, you still need to use the appropriate codes and know the laws regarding who and what is covered in each state. If you see a client for a session while they are on vacation, it is important to check with their insurance company to make sure you will receive payment, or inform your client that they may have to pay out of pocket while they are away. (See interjurisdictional section in chapter 2 for more about state laws.)

As clinicians, we also carry liability insurance. Choosing the provider that can meet the needs of your practice takes some research and some consideration on what you need covered. Just a few years ago, liability insurers had to add a clause that said they would cover video sessions and other forms of technology. However, today it is much easier to obtain coverage for TMH.

Many of the situations I have discussed in this book raise questions as to whether liability insurance would cover the clinician. For example, when a client goes away on vacation in another state and calls for a session, the insurance company may not cover the service due to jurisdiction. The reverse situation can also bring about the same results, such as when a clinician is on vacation in a state where they are not licensed, and they want to continue to serve clients while away.

The best way to ensure liability insurance coverage is to contact the insurance company and discuss any situations where you have questions about coverage. They have qualified professionals to answer your questions and assist you in making good decisions with your TMH practice. Liability insurance is available to keep us protected. As technology changes, we will need to reexamine our coverage to make sure it meets our needs. The more technology we use, the more risks there are, so insurance is necessary. Liability insurers are there to help us, which benefits us now and in the future as technology continues to evolve in our practice.

> *"The whole idea is not about the choice between using or not using technology. The challenge is to use it right."*
>
> —Unknown

6

The Future for Telehealth

In this chapter, I will look at the future of technology for mental health. I will examine some new forms of technology and provide a short discussion on new laws and guidelines in the making, as well as consider new practice guidelines to come.

New Technology

New technology is always forming in someone's mind. We are only limited by our imaginations. As a young person, I never imagined that we would be talking to people face-to-face all over the world with only a click of our phones. I was alive in a time when party lines were used, and smart phones were not a reality. Today, we use technology in almost every area of life. A few years ago, there was great resistance to using technology for mental health, but in light of the COVID-19 pandemic, that has changed. More and more mental health professionals are using technology to meet the needs of their clients, and they are appreciating its many benefits while managing the risks.

In addition, people with serious mental illness are increasingly turning to social media to share their life experiences and obtain advice from those in similar situations (Naslund, Aschbrenner, Marsche, & Bartels, 2016). These online peer-to-peer connections can enhance well-being by promoting feelings of social connectedness and empowering individuals to engage in treatment. Of course, we know there are concerns with the overuse of social media and concerns regarding privacy, but social media has many benefits that continue to grow as technology continues to advance.

Virtual reality (VR) is another form of technology being used to provide treatment. VR uses computer graphics and body-tracking devices along with visual displays and sensory input devices to allow a participant to experience the virtual environment as if it was real life. When I was in peace officer training, we could use a VR video system to make decisions about whether to shoot or not shoot upon entering a room. When I was participating, it seemed as if the situation was really happening. My thoughts were involved, and my body was reacting as if I was there. I also have many young men in my family who play VR games, and when I hear them shouting from the other room or watch them playing, I can tell that it is real life for them in those moments.

Currently, VR is used to train peace officers and military personnel in how to respond to mental health crises, and it is used to train doctors in how to do surgery. VR is also being used in hospitals to treat PTSD. One particular VR game called *BraveMind* simulates the situations a soldier would experience in the battlefield. This VR exposure therapy program has helped many veterans and is now in over fifty hospitals across the United States. VR can be effectively implemented with a competent professional and with a researched program. We need more specialists to take part in this type of research so we can have evidence-based VR practices.

Three-dimensional (3-D) virtual worlds have also been used to create therapeutic environments (Gorini, Gaggioli, Vigna, & Riva, 2008). This method offers anonymous treatment to those who do not want their participation to be known. The participants themselves are not known to one another except by their chosen avatar identity. However, the therapist must assess each participant first and invite only those who are appropriate for the specific groups. This is a valid treatment method to consider for the future of mental health given that it has demonstrated many benefits, such as increased group cohesion and greater therapist-client trust. However, one downfall is that 3-D environments were not created for therapeutic purposes, so clinicians would need to create specific online environments and design them to meet their clients' needs. In addition, 3-D environments are not a form of evidence-based treatment given the lack of research in this area. There is also the possibility of clients becoming addicted to using the virtual world.

In addition, companies are constantly developing and releasing new mental health apps for smartphones, smart watches, and computers that show promise. Increasing numbers of health professionals are also using these apps for mental health care. There are many mental health apps available, ranging from those that help with anger management and mood regulation to those that promote mindfulness practices and stress reduction. When considering apps to use in your practice, continue to look at the risks and benefits of each so you are informed and so your clients know what they are signing up for. The American Psychiatric Association has developed an App Evaluation Model so you can decide if a particular app fits your needs. It is offered on their website, and I have included it here since it gives so much valuable information about using apps: www.psychiatry.org/psychiatrists/practice/mental-health-apps/app-evaluation-model.

New Practice Guidelines

In response to the COVID-19 public health emergency, certain federal privacy regulations were temporarily changed to accommodate the use of technology since in-person sessions were no longer permitted. The Center for Medicare and Medicaid Services expanded their payment policies to include telehealth as an option, and many insurance companies followed by allowing video sessions and even phone sessions under certain conditions. State governors relaxed licensure requirements and altered policies on the provision of services using telehealth. During this time, even HIPAA enforcement was relaxed, and the HHS Office for Civil Rights exercised its "enforcement discretion," meaning that it would not impose penalties for noncompliance with regulatory requirements while clinicians provided services "in good faith."

In light of the changes that were forced upon clinicians, many saw the benefits of using technology that were not evident before. This initiated many mental health professional boards to take a new look at practice guidelines and to quickly make some changes to accommodate this new way of life. At the time of this writing, most changes have been documented as temporary during this global health crisis. However, I believe that within the next year, federal, state, and local guidelines will be reviewed and changed as we move forward with more clinicians deciding to continue providing services to clients via technology.

I have learned that when uncomfortable and seemingly "bad" things happen in my life, it always causes me to look in a direction I may have never looked if that "bad" thing had not occurred. When I am forced to look in this new direction, better things usually present. For example, my job over the last six years has been to travel and present all over the nation, and when the pandemic began, my job ended. After realizing my world was going to be extremely different, I found out about webinars and began presenting my seminars using technology. In addition, because I was at home for two months, I had the time to sit and write this guidebook. Because of all the questions I received every day in my email, I knew this guidebook was needed, so I committed to using my free time to compile the information.

My hope is that those reading this book receive guidance and find resources that will assist you in continuing to help clients with treatment using technology. I also hope that someday I can safely see you all in a live seminar in your hometown. Technology offers us so many options, and many of them are still in our minds. We are only limited by our imaginations when proposing new options. I am excited to see what the next ten years will bring to our field.

> *"Success is liking yourself, liking what you do,*
> *and liking how you do it."*
>
> —Maya Angelou

7

Forms

In this section, you will find examples of forms that I and others have used for mental health practice. Most of them are a combination of many styles and expressions of these forms. Please be advised that these forms are only offered as guidance. When developing these forms, it is best that you consult with a legal advisor or supervisor to ensure that it includes all the important elements for your organization or solo practice. These forms are a guide, not a legal document. For social workers, I have also provided a website in the resource section of this book that includes a suggested informed consent form for TMH. This is a great site for all mental health professionals to consider when preparing to design an informed consent.

You will find the following forms in this chapter:

- Client intake form

- Telemental health informed consent

- Emergency plan

- Authorization for release of information

- Appropriateness assessment

- Sample breach notification letter

Client Intake Form

Please Indicate: Mr. /Mrs. /Ms. /Miss

Marital Status: Single/ Married/ Divorced/ Widowed/ Separated

Client Last Name: _____ First Name: _____ MI: _____

DOB: ____/____/____ Age: _____ S.S.# _____-_____-_____

Street Address: _____

P.O. Box: _____

City: _____ State: _____

Zip: _____-_____

Home Phone: _____

Occupation: _____

Cell Phone: _____

Employer: _____

Work Phone: _____

Employer Address: _____

Is it OK to leave messages at the above numbers? _____

Is it OK to use text messaging? _____

Is it OK to use email messaging? _____

Which email is best to reach you? _____

What is your email address for use with the platform? _____

_____

How did you hear about us? _____

_____

Insurance Information

Person responsible for payment: _____

_____

Address (if different): _____

_____

Home Phone: _____

Cell Phone: _____ DOB: ___/___/___

Occupation: _____

Employer: _____

S.S. #: _____

Employer Address: _____

Primary Insurance: _____

Group #: _____ Policy #: _____

Co-Pay Amount: _____

Client's relationship to responsible party: Self / Spouse / Child / Other

In Case of Emergency

Name of person (not living at same address): _____
_____

Relationship to client: _____

Home/Cell Phone: _____

Client/Guardian Signature: _____

Date: _____

Telemental Health
Informed Consent

I, _____, hereby consent to
participate in telemental health with, _____,
as part of my treatment. I understand that telemental health is the
practice of delivering clinical mental health services using technology
at the two locations where the client and therapist are located at a
distance from each other.

I understand that there are many benefits to using telemental health,
such as convenience, privacy of no office visits, money saved due
no traveling, ease of use, and non-interference of health issues. I
also understand there are risks of using technology that include, but
are not limited to, breaches of confidentiality, privacy issues, and
misinterpretations.

I understand that should a breach occur, my therapist will notify me as
soon as possible. I also understand that if there is a misunderstanding,
my therapist and I agree to communicate with each other as soon
as possible to resolve the concerns. I agree to communicate with my
therapist through the HIPAA-compliant platform that will be used
for video sessions. When this is not possible, emails, text messaging,
and phone calls can be used for contact. All communication will
be returned within two days except on Friday, Saturday, holidays,
and vacations.

I understand there will be no recording of any online session by either
the therapist or myself. All information disclosed in sessions or written
concerning my sessions is considered confidential and will not be
disclosed to any unauthorized person without written permission
except in the case of HIPAA exceptions. These exceptions include when
there is a danger to myself or others, mandatory child and/or elder or
vulnerable adult abuse, or legal proceedings that require disclosure.

I understand that if I am having suicidal or homicidal thoughts, actively
experiencing psychotic symptoms, or having a mental health crisis, my
therapist may determine that a higher level of assistance is needed,
and the appropriate referrals will be made.

I understand that due to the professional code of ethics and to maintain confidentiality, my therapist will not interact with me outside of sessions unless I initiate the interaction. Said interaction will be greetings only and consist of no other engagement of conversation. Further, my therapist will not interact on any social media with past or present clients to maintain ethical compliance.

I understand that my therapist charges $_____ for a _____ - minute session and that this amount is to be paid at the time of the service. I understand that scheduling an appointment requires time to be held open for me; therefore, I agree to contact my therapist _____ hours in advance to cancel, change, or reschedule my appointment. If I choose not to give a _____ hour notice, I understand that I am still responsible for payment of the time scheduled. Since one of the risks of telemental health counseling is disruption in service, should this occur, I agree to use the phone to call my therapist if there is any significant time left in the session. If I choose not to call, I understand that I am responsible for payment of the entire session.

I understand that due to the provision of services from a distance, the use of technology presents limited responses to emergencies. For this reason, my therapist and I will decide on an emergency plan that best suits my needs should an emergency take place during a session. I understand that my therapist may communicate with my emergency contacts in an emergency situation.

I understand that I have the right to withdraw consent and still receive future services.

Print Name: _____

Signature: _____ Date: _____

At the time of the discussion, the client understood the terms and signed without concerns.

Therapist: _____ Date: _____

Telemental Health
Informed Consent

I, _____, hereby consent to
participate in telemental health with _____
as part of my psychotherapy. I understand that telemental health is the
practice of delivering clinical health care services via technology-assisted
media or other electronic means between a practitioner and a client
who are located in two different locations.

1. I understand that there are risks, benefits, and consequences
   associated with telemental health, including, but not limited
   to, disruption of transmission by technology failures, interruption
   and/or breaches of confidentiality by unauthorized persons,
   misinterpretations, and/or limited ability to respond to emergencies.

2. I understand that there will be no recording of any of the online
   sessions by either party. All information disclosed within sessions and
   written records pertaining to those sessions are confidential and may
   not be disclosed to anyone without written authorization, except
   where the disclosure is permitted and/or required by law.

3. I understand that the privacy laws that protect the confidentiality
   of my protected health information (PHI) also apply to telemental
   health unless an exception to confidentiality applies (e.g., mandatory
   reporting of child, elder, or vulnerable adult abuse; danger to self
   or others; I raise mental/emotional health as an issue in a
   legal proceeding).

4. I understand that if I am having suicidal or homicidal thoughts,
   actively experiencing psychotic symptoms, or experiencing a mental
   health crisis that cannot be resolved remotely, it may be determined
   that telemental health services are not appropriate.

5. I understand that during a telemental health session, we could
   encounter technical difficulties resulting in service interruptions. If this
   occurs, I may need to end and restart the session. If we are unable to
   reconnect within ten minutes, please call me at (_____) _____-_____
   to discuss alternative options since we may have to reschedule.

6. I understand that scheduled sessions require payment if not canceled within _____ hours of the start time and that payment is required at the time of service.

7. I understand that my therapist will not interact with past or present clients as part of compliance with the professional code of ethics.

8. I understand that my therapist charges a fee of $_____ per _____- minute session and that payment is to be made at the time of the session.

9. I understand that I have the right to withdraw consent at any time without affecting my right to future care, services, or program benefits to which I would otherwise be entitled.

10. I understand that my therapist may need to communicate with my emergency contacts and/or appropriate authorities in case of an emergency.

_____   _____
Signature of Client   Date

_____   _____
Signature of Therapist   Date

Emergency Plan

Client Name (first and last): _____ Date: _____

Street: _____ City: _____

State: _____ Zip code: _____

Client's Phone: _____ Alternative Phone: _____

Emergency Contact (1): _____

Relationship to Client: _____ Phone: _____

Street: _____ City: _____

State: _____ Zip code: _____

Emergency Contact (2): _____

Relationship to Client: _____ Phone: _____

Street: _____ City: _____

State: _____ Zip code: _____

Local Hospital: _____ Phone: _____

Street: _____ City: _____

State: _____ Zip code: _____

_____ I have provided two emergency contact numbers and the
number to the local hospital or appropriate facility, and my
therapist has permission to communicate with them in
an emergency.

_____ I will always inform my therapist of any changes to my session
location and my emergency contact information at the
beginning of each session.

_____ I have provided a working telephone number to reach me
should the videoconferencing connection fail during a session.

_____ My therapist has provided me with a contact number should
connections fail.

_____   _____

Signature of Client   Date

_____   _____

Signature of Therapist   Date

Emergency Plan

I need to know your location in case of an emergency. You agree to inform me of the address where you are at the beginning of each session. I also need a contact person whom I may contact on your behalf in a life-threatening emergency only. I will only contact this person to go to your location or to take you to the hospital in the event of an emergency.

In case of an emergency, my session location is at the location below:

Address: _____ Phone: _____

City: _____ State: _____

My emergency contact person's name: _____

Address: _____ Phone: _____

City: _____ State: _____

I have read the information provided above and discussed it with my therapist. I understand the information contained in this form, and all my questions have been answered to my satisfaction.

Client signature: _____ Date: _____

Therapist signature: _____ Date: _____

Authorization for Release of Information

Please carefully read the following information before signing this form. If you do not understand the nature of the information to be released, ask your provider. This form should be completely filled out before you sign it.

Name: _____ Date: _____

Birth Date: _____ Social Security #: _____

Street Address: _____ City: _____

State: _____ Zip: _____

I understand that this authorization is voluntary, in my best interest, and not a required condition of treatment.

I understand that my health information may be protected by the Federal Rules for Privacy of Individually Identifiable Health Information (Title 45 of the Code of Federal Regulations, Parts 160 and 164), the Federal Rules for Confidentiality of Alcohol and Drug Abuse Patient Records (Title 42 of the Code of Federal Regulations, Chapter I, Part 2), and/or state laws.

I understand that the release of information is limited to the party named below and that it will not be passed on to anyone else or used for any other purpose other than that specified below.

I understand that my records may contain information regarding my mental health, substance use or dependency, or sexuality, and may contain confidential related information. I further understand that by signing below, I am authorizing the release or exchange of these records to the parties named below.

I understand that I may revoke this authorization at any time by notifying _____ in writing. I understand that revocation does not affect prior action taken under this authorization.

I understand that a photocopy of this authorization is as authentic as the original signed authorization for release of information.

I (full name), _____, authorize
_____ to release and exchange information with:

Name:_____

Agency:_____

Address: _____ Phone:_____

For purpose of: _____

_____

With the following restrictions: _____

_____

From today's date until: _____(date) or one year from today's
date, whichever comes sooner.

Signed: _____ Date: _____

Witnessed: _____ Date: _____

Appropriateness Assessment

These questions may assist you in determining if a client is an appropriate candidate for telemental health. You can make notes on this form and then review the information to make a decision based on their responses and your professional opinion.

- Is there a high risk for emergency care?

- Do they have the cognitive ability to participate?

- Are they physically capable of participating?

- Are they able to hear and speak the available language?

- Is an interpreter necessary?

- Can they read and write in the language used?

- Do they have the technology and equipment necessary?

- Are they competent with the technology?

- Do they have the internet connection needed to support the device or platform?

- Can a safe and private session occur at their location?

- Are they willing to participate?

- Do they have any behaviors that prevent participation?

- Is the presence of a caretaker or other person needed?

- How often do they use technology?

- Do they use it at home or at work?

- What types of technology are they familiar with?

- Do they need training or education to use telehealth?

Sample Breach
Notification Letter

ABC Counseling Services
Street Address
City, State
Zip code

[*Date*]

Re: Personal health information for [*name of victim*]

Dear [*name of victim or representative*],

We are contacting you because we have learned of a serious data security incident that occurred on [*specific or approximate date*] OR between [*date, year and date, year*] that involved some of your personal information.

The breach involved [*provide a brief general description of the breach and include how many records or people it may have affected*]. The information breached contained [*customer names, mailing addresses, credit card numbers, social security numbers, etc.*]. Other information [*bank account PIN, security codes, etc.*] was not released.

We are notifying you so you can take action along with our efforts to minimize or eliminate potential harm. Because this is a serious incident, we strongly encourage you to take preventive measures now to help prevent and detect any misuse of your information. We have advised the three major U.S. credit reporting agencies about this incident and have given those agencies a general report, alerting them to the fact that the incident occurred. However, we have not notified them about the presence of your specific information in the data breach.

To protect you, we have retained [*name of identity theft company*], a specialist in identity theft protection, to provide you with _____ year(s) of [*description of services*] services, free of charge. You can enroll in the program by following the directions below. Please keep this letter because you will need the personal access code it contains in order to register for services.

As a first preventive step, we recommend you closely monitor your financial accounts, and if you see any unauthorized activity, promptly contact your financial institution. We also suggest you submit a complaint with the Federal Trade Commission (FTC) by calling 1-877-ID-THEFT (1-877-438-4338) or online at https://www.ftccomplaintassistant.gov/

As a second step, you also may want to contact the three U.S. credit reporting agencies (Equifax, Experian, and TransUnion) to obtain a free credit report from each by calling 1-877-322-8228 or by logging onto www.annualcreditreport.com.

Even if you do not find any suspicious activity on your initial credit reports, the FTC recommends that you check your credit reports periodically. A victim's personal information is sometimes held for use or shared among a group of thieves at different times. Checking your credit reports periodically can help you spot problems and address them quickly.

You also may want to consider placing a security freeze on your credit files. A freeze prevents an authorized person from using your personal identifying information to open new accounts or borrow money in your name. You will need to contact the three U.S. credit reporting agencies to place the security freeze. The fee is $10 for each credit reporting agency. The agencies may waive the fee if you can prove that identity theft has occurred. Keep in mind that when you place the freeze, you will not be able to borrow money, obtain instant credit, or get a new credit card until you temporarily lift or permanently remove the freeze. To obtain a security freeze, contact the following agencies:

- Equifax: 1-888-298-0045; online: www.freeze.equifax.com
- TransUnion: 1-800-680-7289; online: www.transunion.com (search for security freeze)
- Experian: 1-888-397-3742; online: www.experian.com/freeze.com

If you have further questions or concerns, you may contact us at this special telephone number: 000-000-0000. You can also check our website at www.ourwebsite.org for updated information.

Sincerely,
Marie Copes, LCPC, BC-TMH
ABC Counseling Services

RESOURCES

In this section, you will find many resources that will connect you to the topics I discussed in this guidebook. The following table gives you a way to locate information easily without doing a search. I hope this helps in your continued journey to stay informed.

American Association for Marriage and Family Therapy (AAMFT)	aamft.org
American Association of State Counseling Board (AASCB)	aascb.org
Association of State and Provincial Psychology Boards	asppb.net
American Board of Clinical Social Work (ABCSW) [Formerly the American Clinical Social Work Association (ACSWA)]	acswa.org
American Counseling Association (ACA)	counseling.org
American Counseling Association Licensure Boards	counseling.org/knowledge-center/licensure-requirements/state-professional-counselor-licensure-boards
American Medical Association (AMA)	ama-assn.org
American Mental Health Counselors Association (AMHCA)	amhca.org
American Psychological Association (APA)	apa.org
American Telemedicine Association (ATA)	americantelemed.org
Association for Addiction Professionals (NAADAC)	naadac.org

Boundary Issues in Counseling	counseling.org/Publications/FrontMatter/78090-FM.PDF
Brief Behavioral Activation Treatment for Depression (BATD) Manual	behavioralactivationtech.com/wp-content/uploads/2016/03/Lejuez-et-al_2001.pdf
The Center for Deployment Psychology Lessons Learned Manual	https://deploymentpsych.org/system/files/member_resource/Lessons_Learned_Manual_0.pdf
Coalition for Technology in Behavioral Science (CTIBS)	ctibs.org
Department of Health and Human Services (HHS)	HHS.gov
Dictionary	merriam-webster.com/dictionary/
Duty to Warn Laws	ncbi.nlm.nih.gov/books/NBK542236
HIPAA	HHS.gov/hipaa
HIPAA Telehealth	hhs.gov/hipaa/for-professionals/faq/3015/what-is-telehealth/index.html
HIPAA Security Risk Assessment Tool	healthit.gov/topic/privacy-security-and-hipaa/security-risk-assessment-tool
Indian Health Service (IHS)	ihs.gov
List of Nursing Organizations	nurse.org
Mandated Reporter State Laws	childwelfare.gov/pubPDFs/manda.pdf#page=5&view=Summaries%20of%20State%20laws
Medical Record Documentation Guidelines	https://www.sehealth.org/~/media/files/healthcare-professionals/med-staff-guidelines/policies/medical-record-documentation-and-amendment-guidelines.pdf?la=en
Military One Source	militaryonesource.mil
National Alliance on Mental Illness (NAMI)	nami.org
National Association of Social Workers	socialworkers.org
Office of the National Coordinator of Health Information Technology	healthit.gov
PCI Compliance	pcicomplianceguide.org/faq/

Platform/Software Comparisons	telementalhealthcomparisons.com
Practicing Telepsychology Under PSYPACT	asppb.net/page/telepsychology
Senior Technology	https://mhealthintelligence.com/features/using-telehealth-mhealth-technology-to-help-seniors-age-in-place
Star Providers	Starproviders.org
State Licensing Laws: Center for Connected Health	cchpca.org/sites/default/files/2019-12/LEGISLATIVE%20ROUNDUP%202019%20FINAL.pdf
Telemental Health 50-State Review: Laws, Regulations, Policies	techhealthperspectives.com/2017/10/17/50-state-survey-on-telemental-health-laws-in-the-united-states-2017-appendix-released/
Telemental Health: Legal Considerations for Social Workers	socialworkers.org/About/Legal/HIPAA-Help-For-Social-Workers/Telemental-Health
Telepsychology 50-State Review of Laws and Guidelines	apaservices.org/practice/update/2013/10-24/telepsychology-review
VA Connected Care Program	connectedcare.va.gov
What's Up with Online Therapy Family from *Psychology Today*	psychologytoday.com/us/blog/resolution-not-conflict/201407/whats-online-therapy-and-marriage-counseling

REFERENCES

For your convenience, sample forms are available for download at www.pesi.com/TMH

American Association for Marriage and Family Therapy. (2017). *Best practices in the online practice of couple and family therapy*. Retrieved from https://www.AAMFT.org/Online_Education/Online_Therapy_Guide lines_2.aspx

American Psychiatric Association. (2016). *Telemental health toolkit*. Retrieved from https://www.psychiatry.org/ psychiatrists/practice/telepsychiatry

Cheney, A. M., Koenig, C. J., Miller, C. J., Zamora, K., Wright, P., Stanley, R., ... Pyne, J. M. (2018). Veteran-centered barriers to VA mental healthcare services use. *BMC Health Services Research, 18*(1), 591. https://doi.org/10.1186/s12913-018-3346-9

Duvall Antonacopoulos, N. M., & Serin, R. C. (2016). Comprehension of online informed consents: Can it be improved? *Ethics & Behavior, 26*(3), 177–193. https://dx.doi.org/10.1080/10508422.2014.1000458

Gorini, A., Gaggioli, A., Vigna, C., & Riva, G. (2008). A second life for eHealth: Prospects for the use of 3-D virtual worlds in clinical psychology. *Journal of Medical Internet Research, 10*(3), e21. https://doi.org/10.2196/jmir.1029

Griffiths, K. M., & Christensen, H. (2007). Internet-based mental health programs: A powerful tool in the rural medical kit. *Australian Journal of Rural Health, 15*(2), 81–87. https://doi.org/10.1111/j.1440-1584.2007.00859.x

Gordon, M. S., Carswell, S. B., Schadegg, M., Mangen, K., Merkel, K., Tangires, S., & Vocci, F. J. (2017). Avatar-assisted therapy: A proof-of-concept pilot study of a novel technology-based intervention to treat substance use disorders. *The American Journal of Drug and Alcohol Abuse, 43*(5), 518–524. https://doi.org/10.1080/00952990.2017.1280816

Luxton, D. D., Pruitt, L. D., Wagner, A., Smolenski, D. J., Jenkins-Guarnieri, M. A., & Gahm, G. (2016). Home-based telebehavioral health for U.S. military personnel and veterans with depression: A randomized controlled trial. *Journal of Consulting and Clinical Psychology, 84*(11), 923–934. http://dx.doi.org/10.1037/ccp0000135

Naslund, J. A., Aschbrenner, K. A., Marsch, L. A., & Bartels, S. J. (2016). The future of mental health care: Peer-to-peer support and social media. *Epidemiology and Psychiatric Sciences, 25*(2), 113–122. https://doi.org/10.1017/S2045796015001067

Tomlinson, S. R. L., Gore, N., & McGill, P. (2018). Training individuals to implement applied behavior analytic procedures via telehealth: A systematic review of the literature. *Journal of Behavioral Education, 27*(2), 172–222. https://doi.org/10.1007/s10864-018-9292-0

World Health Organization. (2010). *Telemedicine: Opportunities and developments in member states: Report on the second global survey on eHealth*. Geneva, Switzerland: World Health Organization.

Yuen, E. K., Gros, D. F., Price, M., Zeigler, S., Tuerk, P. W., Foa, E. B., & Acierno, R. (2015). Randomized controlled trial of home-based telehealth versus in-person prolonged exposure for combat-related PTSD in veterans: Preliminary results. *Journal of Clinical Psychology, 71*(6), 500–512. https://doi.org/10.1002/jclp.22168